APOLLO IN THE DEMOCRACY

Walter Gropius

APOLLO IN THE DEMOCRACY

The Cultural Obligation of the Architect

McGraw - Hill Book Company

New York Toronto London Sydney

To my wife Ise Gropius, née Frank,
who selected, translated, and edited the material

Preface

In 1954 I made a trip around the world which put me in the position to compare the development of architecture in South America and in Oriental countries with our own, and, simultaneously, to check my own ideas within the scope of broader aspects.

Most of the articles and lectures collected in this volume originated since then and represent a sort of commentary on the architectural situation of our period. They attempt to clarify the positive and negative results of our incessant search to create an architectural environment for twentieth-century man with which he can identify and which truly corresponds to the rhythm of his life.

Every one of our new discoveries and insights tends to dominate our imagination too exclusively for a while. They need to be scaled down gradually to their actual relative value before they can become incorporated in the general vocabulary and before they can create a new equilibrium on a broader basis. The various trends, fluctuations, and momentary tendencies which influence our total situation always need to be reexamined by our inner compass which protects us against absurdity and exaggeration. The determination not to let this compass slip from our grasp seems to be important in a period which is endangered by overspecialization, for it enables us to see our democratic environment in the totality of its mutual relationships and keeps us from getting too absorbed with sidelines of a purely technical or intellectual order, fascinating as they may be.

The emotional climate of art and architecture swings like an eternal pendulum from the Dionysian pole to the Apollonian, from ecstasy and chaos to self-control and harmony. Even the individual artist seeks to balance these polar opposites in a constant struggle within himself. The Apollo of antiquity was seen as an aristocratic, cultural mentor of princes and the upper classes. He inspired Maecenas. The democracy of the twentieth century, however, will have to replace Maecenas by the cultural will and action of the citizen. Offsetting the materialistic power of technology, he is called upon to reinstate the power of Apollo as a symbol of culture. We are all challenged to help recreate his image.

Walter Gropius

Contents

Apollo in
the Democracy

Address given upon receiving the
"Hansische Goethepreis,"
Hamburg, 1956

Apollo in
the Democracy

My theme, "Apollo in the Democracy," concerns itself with the creation of beauty and with the measure of its reverberations in the democratic society. By the word "democracy" I mean neither the antique Greek form of government which rested upon the power of a comparatively small elite group of free citizens over a solid foundation of slave labor, nor do I mean the politically stressed European, American, or Russian special forms of present democracy. I speak of the form of life which, without political identification, is slowly spreading over the whole world, establishing itself upon the foundation of increasing industrialization, growing communication and information services, and the broad admission of the masses to higher education and the right to vote. What is the relationship of this form of life to art and architecture today?

In a long life I have become increasingly aware of the fact that the

1. Wire sculpture by Richard Lippold, lobby, Pan Am building. *Photo: J. Alex Langley*

creation and love of beauty not only enrich man with a great measure of happiness but also bring forth ethical powers. An age which does not give this love for beauty sufficient room remains visually under-developed; its image remains blurred; and its isolated artistic manifestations find only such limited response that they remain uncharacteristic of the general development.

Man does come into the world with eyes, but only by slow education does he learn to see. Through intensive observation and by growing inner vision his optical imagination is strengthened, enabling him to create genuine form, and by a slow elimination process arrive at artistic standards of value. In our time, with its bookish system of education, the skills of sensual perception have, however, remained undeveloped, and with them the love of beauty. There is a gulf between the public and the creative artist, who is misunderstood and underestimated in his true value, as if he were an expendable luxury member of society, The unprecedented triumphal march of the practical sciences has crowded out the magical in our lives; the poet and the prophet have become the stepchildren of the overpractical man of purpose, who, blinded by the success of mechanized civilization, shuts himself off from them. A pregnant word of Einstein throws light upon the result of this one-sided development: "Perfection of tools, but confusion of aims are characteristic of our time." Long before, Tolstoi had anticipated this cultural dilemma. He accused science of purposely studying "everything." He was of the opinion that mankind could not possibly give its attention to "everything," and that in the attempt to go in a hundred different directions at once, we would tear ourselves to pieces, instead of making clear to ourselves what was most important to us and then declaring this as the goal of our highest aspirations. Tolstoi's challenge is undoubtedly a call for a cultural standard of values upon which we have not come to an agreement to this day.

The intellectual climate prevailing in Tolstoi's time still had a more or less solid, static character, supported by an apparently unswerving faith in the so-called "eternal values." This faith has now yielded to a new concept of a world of unending transformation, of the relativity of all phenomena. The profound changes in our life resulting therefrom have taken place mostly during the last half century of industrial development and have effected in this short period of time a more comprehensive transformation of all human living conditions than the sum of all events of all the centuries since the birth of Christ. The natural inertia of the human heart has not been able to cope with this tempo. The increasing spiritual and intellectual confusion urgently demands a reorientation on the cultural level.

Has not the spiritual direction of mankind's development always been influenced decisively by the thinker and the artist, whose creations stand beyond logical usefulness? To them we must turn anew, for their humanizing influence cannot become effective when society remains indolent and unreceptive. Only where men stand ready to receive the seeds for new cultural growth can these take root and spread. Only where every facet of public life is finally seized by creative forces can a unified social attitude based upon the integrity of the social structure, and which is so indispensable to cultural growth, come into being.

A few generations ago our society was actually still a balanced entity in which every man found his place and where respect for established customs was unquestioned. Art and architecture developed slowly and organically as recognized branches of culture. Society was still all of a piece. Then with the beginning of the age of science and the development of the machine the old social form crumbled. The tools of civilization outgrew us. Instead of leading by moral initiative, modern man developed a mentality which leans mechanistically on quantity instead of quality and serves predominantly utilitarian ends instead of building up a new faith. Every thinking contemporary asks himself doubtfully where the goal of our stupendous scientific progress is to be found. New techniques and new discoveries of ever-faster transportation overtake each other. But what do we do with the time we have gained? Instead of using it for contemplation, for the creative pause, we let ourselves be carried into ever-accelerating haste, fascinated by the idea that "time is money." In his eternal curiosity man has learned to dissect his world with the scalpel of science; but in the process he has lost the feeling for balance and unity. Our scientific age has dulled our perception for the entity of our complicated existence by carrying specialization to the extreme. The professional expert, confused by the profusion of the problems spread out before him, tries to free himself from the pressure of general responsibility by devoting himself to a sharply defined task in a specialized field and refuses to feel responsible for anything outside this restricted area. This has brought about a general dissolution of cultural relationships, resulting in the dismemberment and impoverishment of life. Civilized man has lost his totality. Certain signs indicate, however, that we are slowly moving away from overspecialization with its dangerous atomizing effects upon the inner cohesion of society. If we search the spiritual horizons of today's civilization, we will notice that lately many thoughts and discoveries are aimed exclusively at reconstructing the relationships between the individual phenomena of our world, which the scientists have until now studied only separately, without reference to the neighboring fields. Medicine is building up the psychosomatic concept in the treatment of illness which confirms the mutual interdependence of psyche and soma. Physics has brought forth new recognition of the identity of matter and energy. The artist has learned to express time and motion—the new fourth dimension—with his creative media. Are we on the way toward regaining a more comprehensive idea of this world which we have taken apart? Piet Mondrian points to this "thinking in relationships," away from isolating specialism, in the sentence: "The culture of particular form is drawing to a close; the culture of determined relations has begun."

When we look at our task in its great diversity, we see that it actually embraces the whole life of civilized man in all its essential aspects: the fate of the soil, the forests, the waters, the cities, and landscape; the sciences of man, biology, sociology, and psychology; law, government, economics, art, architecture, and technology. Since all these factors are dependent on one another we may no longer consider them separately. *The will to see relationships is undoubtedly of much greater importance for the planning and shaping of the world around us than all ideas for limited individual solutions, no matter how perfect and practical they may be.* If we agree upon this rank order, then the accent must lie upon a broad "thinking in relationships," which springs from the incessant balancing process in the interplay of forces, in contrast to the thinking of the specialist who purposely never oversteps the boundaries of his limited field.

In our technological society we must passionately emphasize that we are still a world of human beings and that man must stand in his natural surroundings as the center point of all planning and building. Until now, we have so worshiped our new idols, the machines, that we are in danger of losing our spiritual concepts of value. Therefore we should first reexamine the fundamental relationships between man and man, and between man and nature, and not yield to the pressure of special interests or shortsighted enthusiasts who see mechanization as an end in itself. Above all, we must take a more positive attitude in our battle to keep the creative impulses active and effective, as opposed to the deadening mechanization and overorganization within our present democratic society; for our forced and automatized civilization exerts a unique terror all of its own. It is still far from the high democratic goal of bestowing upon man the joys of a life fulfilled. We have not yet found the bond that will hold us together in our endeavor to set up a cultural common denominator strong enough to help us find a form of spiritual expression comprehensible to all.

While our society is aware of the essential importance of the work of the scientist for its continuance, it has apparently forgotten the importance of the creative artist for the form and order of our modern world. In contrast to the processes of mechanization, the work of the true artist consists of an unprejudiced search for a symbolic form of expression of the phenomena of our life. For this he needs the keen unbiased eye of the free man. Since the concept of beauty constantly changes with the development of philosophy and technology, his creativity seeks ever-new nourishment in the scientific and spiritual discoveries of his time and their mutual relationships. His Apollonic work is of the greatest significance for the development of a genuine democracy; for the artist is the prototype of the total man; his freedom, his independence are relatively intact. His intuitive powers are the antidote to our overmechanization; they could give a new balance to our lives and humanize the effects of the machine which still holds us enslaved. *I maintain that our disoriented society desperately needs the creative participation in the arts as an essential counterbalance to the advances of science and industry.*

Experience shows that only in rare cases are cold scientific facts in themselves able to inspire the imagination to such a degree that people are willing to subordinate their fond personal ambitions to a common cause. If people are to be inspired and swept along so that they themselves remove the barriers which today stand in the way of the construction of a more beautiful environment, much deeper chords must be struck than those which can be touched by mere analytical processes. Although scientific progress has brought material abundance and physical wealth, it has not yet been able to give our contemporary civilization that degree of maturity which manifests itself as new form. Our emotional life remains unfulfilled by the purely materialistic production of the eight-hour day. This want of spiritual satisfaction must be the reason for the fact that we have so seldom succeeded in making our brilliant scientific and technical attainments count and the reason why a cultural pattern, such as we should have developed, has hitherto eluded us. *No society of the past ever found its significant expression without the participation of its artists; cultural problems cannot be solved by intellectual processes or political actions alone.* I am speaking here of the great problem of reawakening in every individual the lost ability to create and understand form. But where shall we begin? We need not only the creative artist but also an understanding public. Only by a slow process of education which transmits visual experiences from earliest childhood can we awaken understanding. That is, in kindergarten we must already begin to let the children recreate their environment in imaginative play. Active participation will later become the key to good planning of our environment, since it strengthens the individual's feeling of responsibility, mobilizes his imaginative power, and develops his pride in the self-created environment. An educational concept of this kind would consider theoretical book learning not as an end in itself, but as a help to practical experience which leads to a constructive attitude and way of thought. In every person who has undergone such an educational practice later stimuli toward the improvement of his environment would fall upon fertile ground. As it is, nowadays, we meet instead with a deep-rooted tendency to avoid far-reaching concepts of planning and set down a number of unrelated partial improvements which lack organic cohesion. This can be changed only when a feeling for the whole is carefully taught at every step of the educative process, until it becomes an intrinsic habit to see things in their broader context. When sensitivity to the beautiful has been awakened in us all, a chain reaction might finally occur, creating a common basis upon which extraordinary achievement then may rise. One who keenly realized the necessity of education for the beautiful was Goethe: "That which is useful furthers itself, for the many produce it, and no one can do without it; the beautiful must be furthered, for few create it, and many need it."

The attempt to help regain a cultural balance has dominated my life. The formulation of new concepts of values of suprapersonal significance and the furtherance of group work to broaden the effects: these were my spiritual tools.

The realization of my dream of *total* architecture, embracing the entire visible environment from the simplest utensil to the complicated city, demanded constantly renewed experimentation and searching after new truths in cooperation with other like-minded artists. It represented a program which was meant to lead from observation to discovery, from discovery to invention, and finally to the intuitive shaping of our modern environment. I am proud to report that the basic method of art education, developed by the Bauhaus, has been adopted by an overwhelming number of educational institutions all over the world as an objective means of training varying individual talents.

My experiences during the Bauhaus years led me to a new conception of space in my own architectural work, away from the static space established unchangeably by enclosing walls toward a flowing space sequence, corresponding to the dynamic tendency of our time and seeking to combine the dimensions of space and time in architecture. It became clear to me also that artistic creation draws its life from the tension growing out of the constant reciprocal action between the conscious and unconscious forces of our existence, and that because of this the desired relationship and reciprocity of differing individuals can grow into unity only from within themselves but never as the result of an authoritarian equalization. The attempt at organizing the various visual forms of expression into a kind of "science of form," as the Bauhaus undertook it, has proved the possibility of establishing a solid foundation for spontaneous artistic creation. This serves simultaneously as a key to understanding the various artistic revelations, somewhat like the science of harmony in music. I am speaking of *that* language of form, *Gestaltung,* which is teachable:

the knowledge of optical illusions; the knowledge of the psychological effect of form, color, texture, contrast, direction, tension, and relaxation; and the understanding of what we call the human scale. These are tools for the creative artist who is looking for the humanized standard which, because of its wealth of possible individual variations, corresponds to both the whole and the individual. This objective key to the problem of artistic creation can thus also make it possible for a work group, a team, to synchronize the achievements of its separate members, that is, to begin the important process by which a genuine *Zeitgeist* expression, from the I-cult, can develop.

Has such a spirit already manifested itself in the environment we have built? Only thirty years ago one could count on the fingers of one hand the examples of a future-oriented building concept. Today, the field of vision has broadened. Many beautiful individual works show a common modern expression; but these examples are still isolated and strewn at random across many lands. We have nowhere built the new city of the twentieth century which embodies the life of today as an organic whole, because the spiritual confusion of our hectic time has not yet clarified the social prerequisites for its creation.

It has often been argued that the creator responsible for our environment, the architect, should take society as he finds it and be satisfied to solve his problem aesthetically, so as not to dissipate his strength. This limitation to the creation of beautiful proportions and materials alone is not enough. We have to set our goal much further and build instead an organic setting in which life itself is given a chance and an incentive to *manifest* itself beautifully. Otherwise, our encounter with beauty will remain, as it is today, a rare experience, uncharacteristic of the general level. *Beauty is an integral element of the whole of life and cannot be isolated as a special privilege for the aesthetically initiated; it is a primary need of all.* A feeling for beauty and quality, when it spreads into all levels of society, nourishes the creativeness of the artist and gives him the needed response.

Will modern man reestablish the creative artist in daily life? The artist is always dependent on the sensitivity of his time. His public is always man, not a stratum of art experts. But since no common basis of understanding exists today, he is alone. It will be necessary to find such a unifying basis for our torn world in order that a new culture may again express the dream, wonder, joy, and illusion of human life in new and magical beauty.

The Inner Compass

Address given at seventy-fifth
birthday party, Cambridge,
Mass., May, 1958

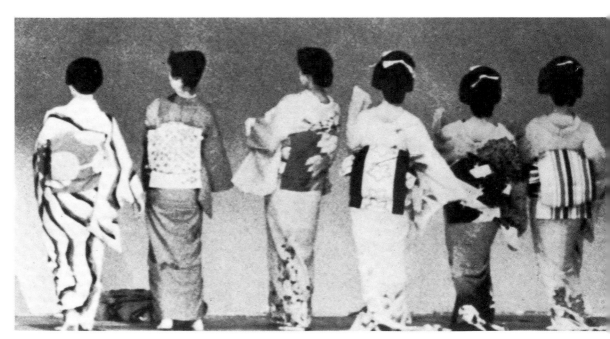

2. Uniforms (West Point Cadets).
Deliberate rigid conformity;
de-individualization of the wearer.
Photo: Life.

The Inner Compass

If there is one real great pleasure in becoming seventy-five years old, it is that you are all here to help me get over the shock. It is quite impossible for me to feel as old as I am, because I have led a triple life—one German, one English, and one American, beginning each one as a neophyte and still learning. It has kept me on my toes, for I had to develop a reliable inner compass to steer me through the pitfalls which my various roles as architectural revolutionary, political *persona non grata,* enemy alien and—most suspect of all—university egghead, provided for me. Now the eggheads have of course been taken out of hiding and are in the process of being dusted off to be shown to the nation in their full glory. But you who have known me as a teacher are pretty well aware of the penalties that go with teaching in this country, and I have had my full share of them in my practice. But there is also a great deal of compensation in teaching, and tonight particularly I

3. Native costumes (Kimono, Sari).
Unity of basic cut, but individual
variation of patterns and
accessories.

think I am entitled to feel proud and happy to see so many alumni of the Graduate School of Design who have made significant contributions to the development of architecture in this country and to applaud them for not having been content to follow the ever-offered recipes for a sure-fire modern architecture, but who have explored the field on their own, independently and courageously. The blight of conformism is the great and present danger of our American life, and I hope you will pit your strength against it. Impatience with the ever-increasing complexity of our responsibilities has tempted too many to give in to a carry-all formula which is supposed to straighten out once and for all the whole field of contradictory demands. But when we look closer, we find that what may look like confusion to the one who still clings desperately to yesterday's formula of dependable eternal truths becomes a source of tremendous inspiration, of never-ending challenge, to the one who has stepped out of the world of static values into the free pattern of relative values and constant transformation. The confusion is not in the manysidedness of the phenomena that are converging on us, but in our inability to relate them to our pattern of living which is still so largely dominated by formulas from the past.

When I came to this country in June 1937, one of my happiest experiences was the healthy curiosity and adventurousness of the American mind. But has not much of this been lost in the meantime? The individual has become timid and often doesn't know how to shake himself free from the ever-tightening embrace of big organization. The technical potentialities have become immeasurably improved, enriched, and refined during his lifetime, but he still uses them awkwardly, hemmed in right and left by real and imagined formulas of the past and of the present. At a moment in history that calls for a bold, imaginative interpretation of the democratic idea, he stands faltering, his mind so occupied with material production that it cannot take flight. Too many of us are still clutching the yardstick of the past, looking anxiously for the protective shelter of an authoritative method. They narrow their choice of expression and their field of experience by docile acceptance of a formula which may have served its initiator well enough, but, used in an imitative approach, leads eventually to formalistic shallowness and an entirely fictitious unity from without.

When, in a world which is still throbbing with the new forces which we have set in motion in the first half of the century, we read or hear that somebody believes to have found *the* solution to a problem, it only shows that he is still rooted in the static conception of yesterday, that he still longs to submit to the dictate of an accepted doctrine. Let us not blame him too much for falling for this old, time-tested way to overcome chaos. However, a democratic cultural unity of our day and age as *I* envisage it cannot result from limitation to dogma and formula, but only from coexistence of all true and vital ideas and their interaction.

Perhaps a concrete example can illustrate this thought. The idea of conquering the complications of modern building by creating flexible, universal space is an intriguing one. But if it were to be tied exclusively to the post and beam method—and then used as a formula by incompetent hands—it would be bound to end in monotony. Technical progress has brought us other constituent elements of form that stir the imagination: the warped plane, the shell which absorbs all forces—compression and tension—in continuity and promises highest performance reached with the least material effort. This newest development is another process of simplification which may lead to the roof becoming the building itself, enclosing universal space, while all the rest is flexible accessories.

Both these approaches, post and beam or warped shells, are true elements of modern architecture. Can we give exclusive preference to the one against the other? No. I think the choice depends on the architect's temperament and inclination and the peculiar set of circumstances he is faced with. Both phenomena will prevail side by side or will be integrated with each other.

There are, however, problems of specific function which cannot be solved within universal space at all, and we should not delude ourselves into accepting it as a panacea for all our troubles. As always, oversimplification is dangerous and tends to evade the stimulating challenge inherent in all new and specific tasks. I agree with a statement made by the Japanese architect Kenzo Tange, who said:

"We should not be trapped by the illusion that we can universalize the function through an abstract grasp of it."

My own approach, from the Bauhaus days on, has always been to shun any formalism and preconceived style idea, but to proceed, instead, empirically, not excluding anything which appears to offer genuine value; to say "and" instead of "either–or," thus seeking *unity in diversity* as the desirable aim. I quote my partner John Harkness, who compares this empirical method with

> . . . the method whereby nature has produced a wide variety of patterns and designs which are constantly modifying themselves to be more adaptable to changing conditions; . . . its workings can be seen, for instance, in the infinite variety and strict order of native costumes all over the world as opposed to the monotony of uniforms which were always the products of dictate and formula. As long as there is a common objective, I believe this approach to hold the greatest promise that the architect of the future may achieve harmony without monotony, order without regimentation.

"As long as there is a common objective. . . ." This is the point where most of our problems arise today. A common objective, welcomed and sustained by broad public support, would in a natural manner call forth many spontaneous individual interpretations and create rich contrasts within a given framework. Lacking ths support, we have as often as not come to accept the substitute of a preconceived formal pattern, superimposed from above, on the living tissue of human activity to achieve at least an external order in place of plain chaos. But such order is of a precarious character, easily uprooted and soon ignored when it remains unabsorbed by life and inexpressive of its real motives. *If we as a people cannot evolve a clearer picture of our common objectives and unite our moral forces behind their realization, the desire of the architect to create unity will go on being thwarted, and his individual contributions toward beauty and order will remain isolated.*

Unity in Diversity

First published under the title
"The Curse of Conformity,"
Sept. 6, 1958,
The Saturday Evening Post,
The Curtis Publishing Co.;
"Deutsche Ubersetzung" in
Bauen und Wohnen

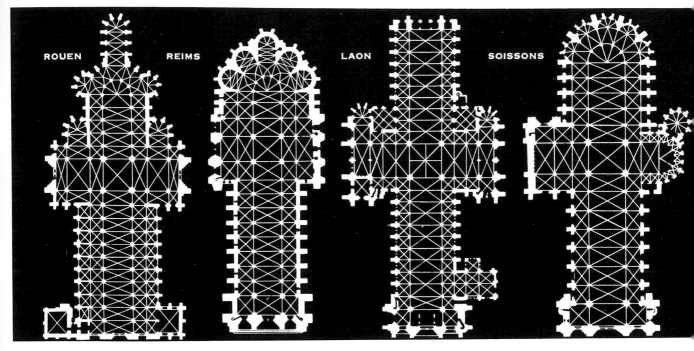

ROUEN   REIMS   LAON   SOISSONS

4. Plans of French Gothic cathedrals. Unity in Variety: repetition
of architectural elements—vaults, buttresses, half-circular
chapels—simultaneously achieves a unified expression of the
period and individual variation in scale and composition.

CHARTRES

Unity in Diversity

From cradle to grave, this problem of running order through chaos, direction through space, discipline through freedom, unity through multiplicity, has always been, and must always be the task of education, as it is the moral of religious philosophy, science, art, politics, and economy.

The Education of Henry Adams

Though American technique is the envy of the world, the "American way of life" does not command unqualified respect abroad. We have proved to all the peoples of the earth that it is possible for an energetic nation to raise its material and civic standards to undreamed-of heights. The example has been zealously studied. Other nations are eager to adopt our magic formula. Yet they are reluctant to accept the idea that the American brand of technology provides the ultimate blueprint for the good life. Indeed, we ourselves are beginning to suspect that economic abundance and civic freedom may not be enough.

Wherein have we failed? In this attempt to analyze some of our shortcomings and to suggest remedies, I draw from my experience as an educator and practicing architect both in this country and abroad. I have also had considerable opportunities to observe the impact of American culture on older countries, especially those which have recently emerged from a feudal or colonial past into the pattern of a modern industrial society. Everywhere the introduction of mechanization has produced such confusion that the problems of the conversion have been more evident than the benefits.

I have become more and more convinced that we have failed to give leadership in the right direction. We have not exported, along with our technical and scientific skills, principles of wise application—mainly because we have not formulated such principles at home. For example, our biggest man-made objects, our cities, have steadily grown more chaotic and ugly, despite brilliant individual contributions to planning and design. For all the heroic efforts of conservationists, a good deal of our loveliest countryside is being bulldozed out of existence, a sacrifice to commercial exploitation. In our smaller towns people try hard to preserve a certain regional character and community spirit—a losing struggle against conformity imposed by mass production. Increasingly, patterns of taste dictated by purely commercial considerations win acceptance, and the natural feeling for quality and appropriateness is dissipated in the giddy tumble from novelty to novelty. The individual is so dazed by the profusion of goods which merchandising propagandists press upon him that he no longer retains much personal initiative or sales resistance.

What should be the goal of our stupendous economic progress? What do we really want to accomplish with our splendid new techniques for faster transportation and wider communication? So far they have merely accelerated our pace without bringing us near enough to our original democratic goal. Instead, the tools of civilization have outgrown us, and their multiplicity has exerted a dominance of its own, a dominance which impairs the individual's capability to seek and understand deeper potentialities. Our subservience to our own brain child, the machine, tends to stifle individual diversity and independence of thought and action—two factors which used to be strong components of the American image. We know, after all, that diversity in unity, not conformity, constitutes the fabric of democracy. Unless we can reconcile diversity with unity, we may end up as robots.

To this world we have transmitted our enthusiasm for new scientific and technical invention; but we worship the machine to such a degree that we have been accused of forsaking the human standards of value

5. School children play "city." In Olga Adams' class in Chicago, school children paint and make models of houses and streets to stimulate their interest in the appearance of their neighborhood.

in its service. Our apologia is that the rapid progress of technology and science has confounded our concepts of beauty and the good life; as a result, we are left with loose ends and a sense of helplessness in the midst of plenty.

We can overcome this defeatism only by understanding that the inertia or alertness of our brain and heart, not the machine, decides our destiny. It is not the tool, it is the mind that is at fault when things get out of hand.

Extreme specialization has dulled our faculty to bring unity to our complicated existence, and this has led to a dissolution of cultural relationships. Consequently, life has become immeasurably impoverished. The spiritual life is being throttled by the all-engulfing rationalism of the "organization man." Man is in danger of losing his entity.

There is only meager evidence that we Americans recognize the urgent task confronting us—to shift the emphasis from "bigger" to "better," from the quantitative to the qualitative, and to give significant form and beauty to our environment. An evolution of this kind would add moral authority to material abundance and would open up frontiers that we have been slow to explore.

Why have we been so hesitant to implement the ideals implicit in the development of our particular way of life? Why does a nation committed to the promise of free universal education take so long to provide enough schools and teachers for its children? Why have we shown so little interest in good housing? And why have we not seen to it that our cities and towns are models of sound organic planning and architectural harmony?

One probable explanation for this last shortcoming is that America's Puritan colonizers, in their preoccupation with the development of an ethical code, paid little attention to the development of an aesthetic code. We are therefore to this day largely dominated by the tenets of a bygone world. The Puritans ignored the fact that aesthetic principles may release ethical powers, and that the codes should have been developed interdependently. The consequent absence in our society of a cultivated sense of beauty has left natural talent underdeveloped and has relegated the artist to an ivory tower.

Where aesthetic standards do prevail in this country, they stem mainly from a preindustrial era—vide our fondness for collecting antiques. But there can be no true relation between the artistic inspiration of that era and the present requirements of a mass audience.

These requirements have not been satisfied by the material production of the eight-hour working day. We are beginning to realize that two important ingredients—beauty and inner resourcefulness—are missing in our brave new world. Cultural problems cannot be solved by intellectual processes only. We must go down to the roots to reawaken in every individual the ability to understand and create form.

How can such a renascence be achieved in a society almost exclusively devoted to commercial exploits and the accumulation of factual data? This may seem a strange question to ask in a country that fosters so many institutions designed to preserve art treasures and to encourage artistic activities. It is true that these institutions—the museums, art associations, and foundations—perform a valuable service, but they can do no more than impart "art appreciation" to those who feel they can afford what they consider a luxury. They exert little influence on schools, where art is of secondary importance to the study of English, history, and mathematics.

At one time, standards of taste were imposed through power or example by the leading feudal caste. Later on the business tycoons, for better or worse, influenced others to follow their personal preferences or whims. Our generation takes its cultural guidance from groups of their fellow citizens—school boards, city councils, women's clubs—chosen by popular consent to make important cultural decisions. This is as it should be, for democratic principles not only permit but demand that each individual bring his personal conviction and insight to bear upon his surroundings.

But how have these citizens trained themselves to deserve confidence in their judgment? How have they learned to distinguish between diversity and anarchy, between organic planning and mere accumulation? We assume too much if we expect them to function properly in this role without having had a chance to develop powers of discrimination. They must first be made aware of the possibilities of promoting a stimulating environment for themselves and their community rather than resorting to clichés or pinchpenny expediency. As it is, their education rarely leads to a grasp of organic development and visual beauty. The pseudoartistic examples of design that reach them through aggressive sales techniques, with their competitive assault of chaotic shapes and colors, is apt to reduce them to a state of sensorial apathy.

We need to revitalize our natural creative capacities which for so long have been allowed to atrophy. It will not, of course, be easy to recapture a birthright almost completely forsaken. The effort must begin in school, during the child's formative years.

To accomplish this, our educational system, with its overemphasis on fact-finding, must cultivate attitudes which will integrate emotional experience with scientific and technical knowledge. The strong puritan bias in our national origin, mistrustful of emotional responses, has so influenced education that natural impulses have been inhibited and the artistic imagination cannot take wing. We must overcome such prejudices and broaden our educational approach to include the recognition of emotional impulses, controlling rather than suppressing them.

The development of our imaginative faculties would then generate an atmosphere in which the artist could flourish not as an isolated phenomenon, ignored or rejected by the crowd, but as an integral part of our public life.

We already let our children in kindergarten recreate their surroundings in imaginative play. This interest, in one form or another, should be intensified and perpetuated all the way through school and college. Practical design problems in form, color, and space relations should be studied and actual materials used for their representation. In such an educational concept I do not view book learning as an end in itself, but rather as a means to illuminate practical experience. It should become second nature for the student to adopt a constructive attitude toward the appearance of his own habitat so that in later life he may creatively participate in its development.

Nothing promotes an understanding of environmental planning better than active participation in it. If such a general spirit penetrates society at all levels, the artistically gifted will then respond naturally and exuberantly, giving expression to the common desire. The artist's work and message will be understood by all people, not just by one group or clique.

6. American street scene, 1965. Confusing chaos of "Main Street."
Photo: Bill Ray, Life.

The modern artist is frequently accused of moving in an exclusive world of his own, a stranger to his fellow men. But a true artist is always a candid interpreter of his society. If his society has few clear aims and standards, his work will reflect that lack. Instead of condemning him if he does not produce soothing entertainment, we should heed and try to understand his message. The interpretation of beauty constantly changes with the development of philosophy and science, and as the artist is sensitive to the spiritual and scientific concepts of his time, he intuitively expresses them. If we cannot always follow him, the fault may lie in our complacency toward the very forces that shape our times. There is no cause to berate the artist for deliberate mystification or frivolity when we, his audience, have lost interest in his search for a symbolic expression of contemporary phenomena. Our society desperately needs his stabilizing influence to moderate the furious tempo of science and industry.

What kind of educational climate must we provide to fire the imagination of a potential artist and equip him with an infallible technique?

Out of a passionate concern with this problem, realizing that the lone "visionary" had little chance to change the general education or industrial system, I took it upon myself almost forty years ago to found a pilot institute. This was the Bauhaus School of Design in Weimar and later Dessau, Germany. The faculty, whom I recruited from the ranks of the most advanced painters, sculptors, and architects of the day, and I shared the belief that it was essential to select talented young people before they had either surrendered to the conformity of the industrial community or withdrawn into ivory towers. We proposed to train them to bridge the gap between the rigid mentality of the businessman and technologist and the imagination of the creative artist. We wanted our students to come to terms with the machine without sacrificing their initiative, so that they might bring to mass production, to architecture, and to community planning a sense of order and beauty.

To that end we combined our efforts to evolve a teachable, supra-individual language of form based on psychological and biological factors. This language was to furnish the student with an objective knowledge of visual facts. Beyond that, it was to establish a common background for spontaneous artistic creation, saving the work of the artist from arbitrariness or isolation and making it part of the development of a genuine *Zeitgeist,* away from the I-cult. Our object was not to supply a new set of recipes, but to inculcate a new set of values reflecting the thought and feeling of our time. That goal could be approached only by an unfettered search for the laws governing materials and techniques as well as those governing human psychology. Our students were first taught the psychological effects of form, color, texture, contrasts, rhythm, light, and shade. They were familiarized with the rules of proportion and human scale. They were encouraged to explore the fascinating world of optical illusions, indispensable to the creation of form. The student was led through many stages of creative experience with various materials and tools to make him aware of their potentialities as well as his own talents and limitations.

After this basic course the students were trained in a specialized craft of their own choice. The instruction in craftsmanship given in the Bauhaus workshops was not an end in itself, but a means of education. The aim was to turn out designers able, by their intimate knowledge of materials and working processes, to produce models for industrial mass production, which were not only designed but made at the Bauhaus. These designers had to be fully acquainted with the methods of production on an industrial scale and so, during their training, they were assigned temporarily to practical work in factories. Conversely, skilled factory workmen came to the Bauhaus to discuss the needs of industry with the staff and the students.

The Bauhaus was not concerned with producing designs of ephemeral commercial gadgets. It was rather a laboratory for basic research into design problems of all types. Staff and students succeeded in giving their work a homogeneity based not on external, stylistic features, but on a fundamental approach to design which resulted in standard products rather than novelties.

In short, the purpose of the Bauhaus was not to propagate any style, system, or dogma, but to exert a revitalizing influence on design. We sought an approach to education which would promote a creative state of mind and thus help to reestablish contemporary architecture and design as a social art.

The influence of the Bauhaus on American design and design curricula has been widespread. Its lesson is particularly applicable in this country because nowhere else is the assembly-line method so firmly entrenched and, consequently, nowhere does a greater need exist for a guide to standards of excellence in mass production. A firm resolve to mass-produce goods of both technical quality and cultural significance would have far-reaching effect because the world has learned to watch the United States for signposts to where the journey into the machine age is heading. So far, the rest of the world has been thrilled by some of the achievements of United States designers and manufacturers, but more often it has been merely snowed under by an avalanche of poorly designed gadgets, the modish fluctuations of an industry bent on attracting customers by entertainment value rather than by quality. Respect for a sound standard product, combining function with aesthetic value, is at a low ebb. Merchandising catchwords attempting to glorify every trifling industrial product have beclouded the issue. There is no sustained effort to determine which features of our vast industrial civilization represent the best and lasting values and should therefore be cultivated to form the nucleus of a new cultural tradition for the machine age. Instead of recognizing that cultural achievement stems from the selection of the essential and typical, we exalt quantity.

Selectivity is a criterion of a balanced culture. Indiscrimination leads to cultural anarchy. To achieve true standards, we must first cultivate a voluntary discipline, acknowledging that there is greater excitement and promise of beauty in purposeful limitation than in mere accumulation. Variety for variety's sake as a continuous national program will eventually surfeit even the most voracious consumers and alienate our warmest admirers abroad.

The idea of limitation has never greatly appealed to Americans. Early in their history they embarked on the ambitious plan of proving that material blessings could be shared by all. But having largely accomplished this we must now open new doors. One of the brightest prospects will be the creation of visual order out of our chaotic modern scene by cooperative efforts and coordinated planning.

Obviously, the ideas which finally crystallize into an aesthetic principle must be rooted in society as a whole, not in individual genius alone. *But it is a common background of distinct attitudes that the artist needs to relate his own contribution successfully to an established social order.* In all great cultural periods unity of form has been given to the man-made environment. This, in retrospect, we call "style." To reach this goal, we must restore the influence of the artist. We must establish him in our industrial framework as a full-fledged member of the production team along with the engineer, the scientist, and the businessman. Only together can they combine low cost, good technique, and beautiful form in our products. Initiative in business must be balanced by initiative in cultural fields. *To become fully mature a democracy must bestow the highest prestige upon the artist.*

The American sophisticate roams the world today nostalgically searching for products that do not bear the stamp of mass production and sales organization. This is a sentimental journey to recover what he has lost at home. He seeks standard products whose usefulness and beauty have been patiently developed by the skill and unwavering good sense of generations of craftsmen, and which, ironically, have now become curios for connoisseurs. The thrill of acquisition grows rarer as economic pressures force other countries to remake them-

8. Plaza and streets in Venice. Successful
arrangement of the urban living space, its plaza
and its surrounding buildings. Surprise effects
from one open space to another. The pedestrian
prevails.

selves in the American image of mechanical mass production. Meanwhile, whoever turns his back on his own civilization forfeits the chance to perform a service which his heritage, his basic philosophy, and present need urgently demand of him—namely, to turn the calamities of the machine age into assets by inculcating the desire for quality and beauty in the producer as well as in the consumer.

As long as our "cultured" elite insist that undiscriminating popular taste is beyond repair, that salvation lies only in imposing upon an uncomprehending public an authoritative aesthetic formula, they will sidestep the particular obligation of a democratic society—to work from the ground up instead of from the top down. The dicta of the illuminati derive from an epoch when cultural matters were the concern of an elite who could enforce standards of taste, as well as of production. This cannot suffice in our present democratic system. *A social organization that has conferred equal privileges on everybody must finally acknowledge its duty to prevent such privileges from being wasted through ignorance and unresponsiveness.* This can be accomplished only by gradually raising the general level of perceptiveness and discrimination, not by handing down formulas from above. Aesthetic creativeness cannot survive either as the privilege and occupation of an esoteric few or as an embellishing cloak thrown over the unlovely features of the contemporary scene. It should be a primary function of all, with a solid foundation in popular custom. *Unity in diversity*—the symbol of culture and its sublime manifestation.

The next generation may witness such a unification of society. The role of the artist will then be to find the humanized image for society's aspirations and ideals. By virtue of his ability to give visible symbols to significant order, he may once again become society's seer and mentor and as a custodian of its conscience solve the American paradox.

The Tree of Life
versus the Sales Spiral

Address given upon receiving the
Albert Medal by the Royal Society
of Arts, London, Nov. 9, 1961

The Tree of Life
versus the Sales Spiral

Since this concerns the development in theory and practice of an idea which began taking shape in my mind fifty years ago, I should be able to reminisce on the ups and downs, the victories and defeats this idea encountered during its slow but steady growth. But I am a very poor prospect in this respect, for, to this day, I have been unable to recapitulate and reassess my own life in a biography, mainly because I have been too busy living it. I also have my doubts whether anybody looking back on his own history can truly relate the impact of events on his mind or, conversely, the impact his mind had on events. After all, he has reached another phase of life; he lives in a changed emotional climate, and his present vision is conditioned by new experiences, new horizons.

For instance, some time ago I was visited by a German art historian who is in the process of writing a detailed and well-documented ac-

9. The Royal Society of Arts, London.

count of the Bauhaus years between 1919 and 1928. In the course of our searching through old files, we came upon a diary my wife had kept throughout the last six years in Weimar and Dessau and which we had not reexamined since. I began reading it, and the further I proceeded the more I became depressed, for it became perfectly clear to me from the text that of all the tremendous effort put into that enterprise, 90 percent had gone toward fighting the hostile forces of the local and national environment, and less than 10 percent had been spent on creative work. Mind you, the depression I *now* experienced at this discrepancy had never been felt at the time, except for short intervals; it was only in retrospect that the overwhelming odds against the continuation of an institution, dedicated to a completely unorthodox, revolutionary approach to design, became fully apparent. While we were at it we knew perfectly well that we had to wrest every bit of our existence from the lion's mouth, but we never doubted our strength to overcome opposition. We were fighting mad at being hampered in our work; but we were not depressed. We felt we were standing at a new beginning and had accomplished only the first few steps into a newly discovered world full of challenges and promises.

Armed with my present knowledge, I would have said that it could *not* be done, that the interlude between the end of World War I and Hitler's advent was much too short to accomplish anything of lasting value, that the long hibernation into which all creative minds were forced during the Nazi years would surely have killed off the carefully sown seed. And yet, here I am, twenty-eight years after my exodus from Germany, picked out by you as the representative of all those who weathered those early years with me, to receive your highest prize for leadership in design.

So, don't you ever believe an old man when he says that something cannot be done; he cannot possibly put himself back into the shoes of a young man who simply goes to work, confidently setting the stage as if he were going to live forever. It is only by this stretch of his imagination that he can thrust his thoughts ahead far enough to outlast his lifetime.

Well, whatever did become possible during those hard-pressed years when teachers and students at the Bauhaus worked in a kind of collaboration which had never been tried before, has now been concentrated in the newly created Bauhaus Archiv in Darmstadt, Germany, with the Prinz zu Hesse und Rhein as President and supported by the Bonn Government and by the City of Darmstadt. There all the documents and quite a few of the original products have been brought together to allow those interested in the development and the subsequent spread of this movement to get a firsthand glimpse at it. I had collected all comments made in the press, hostile and otherwise, at the time, and this alone provides an interesting study of the climate of the twenties and thirties and the resulting political and cultural interaction. Legend has thereby been transformed into comprehensible reality and doesn't have to rely any more on individually biased reminiscences of the participants or on hearsay. To me, personally, it has come as a great relief to be able to refer interested scholars, educators, and artists to this collection of source material, since I have found it increasingly difficult to have to give constantly evidence about my past while I am still so involved with the present.

The Bauhaus Archiv itself, of course, does not want to confine its task only to the documentation of its own past and its later influence on others, but endeavors to become a center for the study of living art, architecture, and design through exhibitions, books, and lectures.

You may wonder how these ideas can make their way today in a period which, far from being dominated by the artist, does not even reflect the desires of the manufacturer, nor for that matter the public demand, but is characterized by the power of the sales propagandist, of what your Mr. Toynbee calls the "Tempter" or what in the United States are called "The Madison Avenue boys." Under this regime it seems completely futile to inject quality into buildings and goods which are created only for their short entertainment value before they are discarded or exchanged for another set of equally ephemeral items.

I remember how struck I was by this, our modern predicament, when, during my visit in Japan, I entered a Tokyo department store and found myself presented with two entirely different sections: one was the traditional yard goods display, the other the center for modern fabrics, created for the modern women of Japan. The discrepancy between the two was staggering. The first one was filled with an endless variety of excellently designed patterns, any one of which I could have bought blindfolded because there wasn't a bad one among them.

The second one was filled with the haphazard output which we know so well from our own stores, where quality of design is strictly accidental and often not higher priced than indifferent or bad design. Since in the past the Japanese customer had obviously been exposed to a selection of the very best, it seemed incomprehensible that their modern designers should suddenly be satisfied with turning out such inferior and uneven work. The explanation is, of course, that in former times the vast majority of the buying public knew how to choose from the big reservoir of tried and true patterns which was only so slowly increased that no half-baked work had a chance to get by in the elimination process. It takes discipline, discrimination, and an instinct for quality on the side of the customer as well as of the designer to bring about such a high standard of work, and it is this interplay between the creative artist and an understanding public which is missing in our world today. The fast change from an evenly high level of design in Japan to the uncertain, groping, perpetually experimental approach of the Western world shows that even such a highly gifted and trained people as the Japanese cannot successfully cope with the pressure of the modern sales campaign which has so completely upset the slow, discerning, knowledgeable ways of the past.

Can we extricate ourselves from this merry-go-round and supply the young generation with the resilience, the independent judgment, and the moral stamina which would enable them to rise above the cloud of the fake values which is smothering us?

You may say that I am repeating myself when my answer is again: more intensified education. We cannot hope, at this point, to regain lost ground by expecting gradual improvement to come from the slow-moving, natural adjustment of human nature to the impact of events; events have a tendency these days to run us down faster than we can respond to them unless we manage to make education into a force that does not only sharpen and illuminate the mind, but also forms the sensibilities and guides eye and hand as well. This kind of education we had until now reserved for the artist; but if we cannot give it to everybody, the gulf between him and the people will remain unbridged. If we congratulate ourselves today on the strides that have been made in releasing the young artist from the bondage in which he was formerly held by having to follow the methods and recipes of his teacher, we must realize that the greater part of the task is still before us: namely, to give to the average young person, right from the beginning of his schooling, a visual training based on objective principles, i.e., on the laws of nature and the psychology of man. Standing on such a sound foundation, the gifted individual will find his personal interpretation; but artists and public alike must start out from the same premises of universal validity. Only then will creativity of the maker find the response of the user.

For me there isn't much more time left to carry on this work, but I hope that England, the most mature country of the Western world, and most conscious of the great power of education, will produce men who will eventually blaze a trail out of the commercial jungle in which we are entangled; for it seems to be unimaginable that human nature should not eventually rebel against the conspiracy to replace the "tree of life" with a sales spiral.

**The Role of the Architect
in Modern Society**

Address given upon receiving the
degree of Doctor of Humane Letters
from Columbia University,
March, 1961

The Role of the Architect in Modern Society

I should like to talk about the ambiguous position of the architect in his relation to society and about his double role as a citizen and a professional. I want to point out why he, armed with an arsenal of intricate technical means, design theories, and philosophical arguments, so rarely succeeds in pulling his weight in the realm of the public domain where decisions are made which vitally affect his interests. Since popular opinion holds him responsible for the appearance of our cities, towns, and countryside, I would like to examine his position in this respect and which avenues of action are open to him to broaden his influence.

I would like to add also my reactions to certain "rumbles" in the architectural profession which have been growing in intensity. Since

10. Redwood City, California, project model.
Norman C. Fletcher (The Architects Collaborative).
Combination of town houses with walk-ups and
highrise apartment buildings avoids monotony.
Photo: Phokion Karas, Melrose, Mass.

architects possess, in general, a sensitive, built-in thermometer which registers the crises and doubts, enthusiasms and fancies of their contemporaries, we should listen to the notes of misgiving, warning, or satisfaction emerging from their quarters.

All reports made lately by architects and educators on the state of architecture in the sixties were dominated by two words: *confusion* and *chaos.* It seems to them that the inherent tendencies of an architecture of the twentieth century as they were born fifty years or so ago and appeared then as a deeply felt, indivisible entity to their initiators, have been exploded into so many fractions that it becomes difficult to draw them together to coherence again. Technical innovations, first greeted as delightful, new means to an end, were seized separately and set against each other as ends in themselves; personal methods of approach were hardened into hostile dogmas; a new awareness of our relationship to the past was distorted into a revivalist spirit; our financial affluence was mistaken for a free ticket into social irresponsibility and art-for-art's sake mentality; our young people felt bewildered rather than inspired by the wealth of means at their disposal and were either trying to head for safe corners with limited objectives or succumbing to a frivolous application of kaleidoscopically changing patterns of "styling" or "mood" architecture. In short, we are supposed to have lost direction, confidence, reverence, and everything goes.

When trying to respond to the situation, I would like first of all to extricate myself from the verbal jungle we have gotten ourselves into. What actually is chaos? One definition is: "A state of things in which chance is supreme." Well, those of us who feel bewildered by "chaoticism" may take comfort from the fact that the ancient Greeks considered Chaos to be the oldest god of all times.

Personally I do not feel too fearful of this god, who returns periodically to stir things up on earth; for never during my life-span has the architectural mission looked any less dangerous, difficult, or chaotic to me as it does now. It is true that in the beginning of the struggle the battle lines were drawn more clearly, but the fight was essentially the same: the coming to terms of a romantically orientated, jealously individualized architectural profession with the realities of the twentieth century. It seems to me that the specter of confusion is haunting mostly those who, for a short while, thought they had won all the battles and found all the answers, those who have come by their inheritance too easily, who have forgotten the great goals set at the beginning and now find their equilibrium upset by new developments in the social and technical field.

But let me examine the meaning of the word "chaos" more closely in all its aspects.

With our tremendously accelerated communication system, it has become quite easy today for people in all corners of the world to reiterate the most advanced ideas *verbally* while actually being unable to catch up with themselves in this respect *emotionally.* Therefore, we see all around us an astonishing discrepancy between thought and action. Our verbal glibness often obscures the real obstacles in our path which cannot be sidestepped by brilliant and diverting oratory. It also creates too rosy an impression of the actual influence architects are permitted to take in the shaping of our larger living spaces. Whether a conscientious and dedicated architect of today resolves his personal design problem in this or that way is, unfortunately, less decisive for the general appearance of our surroundings than we are fond of believing. His contribution is simply swallowed up in the featureless growth that covers the acres of our expanding cities. In the last twenty years the United States has seen the emergence of an unusual number of gifted architects who have managed to spread interest and admiration among designers in other countries. But when the curious arrived at our shores to see the new creations for themselves, they were overwhelmed by the increase in general ugliness that hit their eyes before they even had a chance to find the objects of their interest in the vast, amorphous display. It is here where chaos reigns supreme; it is the absence of organic coherence in the total picture which causes the disappointment, not the dilemma between different individual approaches to design.

Having been in the crosscurrents of architectural development for over half a century now, I find that an architect who wants to help mold the evolutionary forces of his time instead of letting himself be overcome by them must distinguish between two sets of components which are apt to influence and direct his work. The first one consists of the human trends which gradually move a society toward new patterns of living; the second consists of the contemporary technical means and the individual choices of form expression which help these trends to take shape. It is imperative never to lose sight of the first while getting embroiled with the second, because the architect is otherwise in danger of losing himself in the design of technical stunts or in personal mannerisms.

The potentialities of the new technical means fascinated my generation just as much as they do the architect of today, but at the beginning of our movement stood an idea, not an obsession with specific forms and techniques. The activities of life itself were under scrutiny. How to dwell, how to work, move, relax, how to create a life-giving environment for our changed society; these were what occupied our minds. Of course, we went about the realization of such aims in very different ways, but I do not see why this diversity should by itself cause confusion, except to those who naïvely believe that there is always only one perfect answer to a problem. There are, of course, many technical and formal approaches to the same task, and any one of them may be successful if it is well suited to the purpose of the building, to the temperament of the architect, and if it is used with discrimination in its given environment.

The great technical inventions and social developments of the last hundred years which set off such a stream of changes in our way of living and producing gradually established new habits, new standards, new preferences which have come to represent the unifying trends in today's general picture. Beginning with the discovery of the Bessemer steel and of Monier's reinforced concrete which freed architecture of the supporting, solid wall and presented it with virtually limitless possibilities for flexible planning, there has been a steady movement toward a less rigid, less encumbered style of living and building. The skeleton structures enabled us to introduce the large window opening and the marvel of the glass-curtain wall—today misused and therefore discredited—which transformed the rigid, compartmental character of buildings into a transparent "fluid" one. This, in turn, gave birth to a totally new dynamic indoor–outdoor relationship which has enriched and stimulated architectural design beyond measure. Pressure for ever-more mobility and flexibility encouraged the evolution of industrial prefabrication methods which have, by now, taken over a large part of our building production, promising ever-increasing precision and simplification of the building process for the future. The common characteristics which clearly emerged from all these innovations are: an increase in flexibility, a new indoor–outdoor relationship, and a bolder and lighter, less earthbound architectural appearance. These are the constituent elements of today's architectural imagery, and an architect can disregard them only at his peril. If related to a background of meaningful planning, they would reveal diversity, not chaos.

I cannot accept, therefore, the verdict of the critics that the architectural profession as such is alone to blame for the disjointed pattern of our cities and for the formless urban sprawl that creeps over our countryside. As we well know, the architect and planner has almost never received a mandate from the people to draw up the best possible framework for a desirable way of life. All he usually gets is an individual commission for a limited objective from a client who wants to make his bid for a place in the sun. It is the people as a whole who have stopped thinking of what would constitute a better frame of life for them and who have, instead, learned to sell themselves short to a system of rapid turnover and minor creature comforts. It is the lack of a distinct and compelling goal rather than bad intentions of individuals that so often ruins attempts of a more comprehensive character to general planning and sacrifices them bit by bit to the conventional quick-profit motive.

And this is, of course, where we all come in. In our role as citizens we all share in the general unwillingness to live up to our best potential in the lack of dedication to our acknowledged principles, in our lack of discipline toward the lures of complacency and material abundance.

Julian Huxley, the eminent biologist, warned only recently that "sooner rather than later we must get away from a system based on artificially increasing the number of human wants and set about constructing one aimed at the qualitative satisfaction of real human needs, spiritual as well as material and physiological. This means abandoning the pernicious habit of evaluating every human project solely in terms of its utility. . . ."

Our cunning sales psychology, in its unscrupulous misuse of our language, has brought about such a distortion of truth, such a dissolution of decency and simple honesty, not to speak of its planned wastefulness, that it is high time for the citizen to take to the barricades against this massive onslaught against the unwary. Naturally, the all-pervading sales mentality has also had its detrimental effect on the architecture of our time. Relentless advertising pressure for ever-changing, sensational design has discouraged any tendency to create a visually integrated environment because it tacitly expects the designer to be different at all cost for competition's sake. The effect is disruptive and quite contrary to the desirable diversity of design which would result naturally from the work of different personalities who are aware of their obilgations to environmental integration. Here again we see that the forces which cause confusion and chaos originate from the excessive infatuation with the rewards of salesmanship which dominates modern life and which we can influence only in the role of human beings and democratic citizens, but hardly as professionals.

I was somewhat startled, therefore, by a remark in the recent AIA Report on the state of the profession: "The total environment produced by architecture in the next forty years can become greater than the Golden Age of Greece, surpass the glories of Rome and outshine the magnificence of Renaissance. This is possible provided the architect assumes again his historic role as Masterbuilder."

How does this vision compare to the realities of the situation at hand? Don't we need to remember that such high points in history came about only when the skill and artistic inspiration of the architect and the artist were carried into action by the clear and unquestioned authority of those who felt themselves to be the rightful representatives of a whole people? The Greek pinnacle was reached by the courage and foresight of their leader, Pericles, who pulled together all financial and artistic resources of the whole nation and its allies, including the military budget, to force the erection of the Parthenon. The Romans, spreading this Mediterranean heritage over the whole of the Roman empire, set in their buildings monuments to the centralized power of their leaders. The Renaissance, after giving birth to fierce political rivalry, harnessed all secular and clerical powers, all craftsmen and artists, for the glorification of the competing principalities. Wherever we look in history, we find that the rulers took no chances with the individual tastes and inclinations of the populace, but imposed strict patterns of behavior as well as a hierarchy of religious, civic, and economic standards which dominated architectural and artistic expression. In Japan this even covered the proportionate size of all domestic architecture, which was strictly regulated according to birth, rank, and occupation of the owner.

All these systems have produced magnificent results in one period or another, but they no longer have roots in our modern world. Even if some authoritative remnants are still around in the form of large corporations and institutions, this cannot conceal the fact that the architect and artist of the twentieth century has to face a completely new client and patron—the average citizen or his representative whose stature, opinion, and influence are uncertain and difficult to define compared to the authoritarian lord of the past. As we have seen, this citizen, as of now, is not at all in the habit of extending his vision beyond his immediate business concerns, because we have neglected to educate him for his role of cultural arbiter. He repays this neglect by running loose, only here and there restricted by social ambitions from recklessly following his commercial interests. Though he is quite aware of the restrictions the law puts on his building activities, he is almost totally unaware of his potentialities to contribute something positive, socially and culturally, to the actual development, change, and improvement of his environment. So far we are trying only to prevent him from committing the worst abuse; but I feel that unless we take the positive step of trying to mold him into the man of responsibility he must become, there will be little chance for the "masterbuilder" ever to assume again his comprehensive historic role as creator of cities.

Our modern society is still on trial where cultural integration is concerned. It certainly cannot be accomplished by handing out authoritative beauty formulas to an uncomprehending public, untrained to see, to perceive, to discriminate. *A society such as ours, which has conferred equal privileges on everybody, will have to acknowledge its duty to activate the general responsiveness to spiritual and aesthetic values, to intensify the development of everybody's imaginative faculties. Only this can create the basis from which eventually the creative act of the artist can rise, not as an isolated phenomenon, ignored and rejected by the crowd, but firmly embedded in a network of public response and understanding.*

The only active influence which our society can take toward such a goal would be to see to it that our educational system for the next generation will develop in each child, from the beginning, a perceptive awareness which intensifies his sense of form. Seeing more, he will then comprehend more of what he sees and will learn to understand the positive and negative factors which influence the environment in which he finds himself. Our present methods of education, which put a premium on accumulation of knowledge, have rarely reached out to include a training in creative habits of observing, seeing, and shaping our surroundings. The apathy we meet in many citizens, who entertain only vague notions of wishing "to get away from it all," can certainly be traced to this early failure to arouse their active interest in the improvement of their living areas. Children should be introduced right from the start to the potentialities of their environment, to the physical and psychological laws that govern the visual world, and to the supreme enjoyment that comes from participating in the creative process of giving form to one's living space. Such experience, if continued in depth throughout the whole of the educational cycle, will never be forgotten and will prepare the adult to continue taking an informed interest in what happens around him. Recent research at the University of Chicago has shown that "the high I. Q. children seek out the safety and security of the 'known,' while the high creative children seem to enjoy the risk and uncertainty of the 'unknown.'" We should strengthen this creative spirit, which is essentially one of nonconformist, independent search. We must instill respect for it and create response to it on the broadest level, otherwise the common man stays below his potential and the uncommon man burns up his fireworks in isolation.

My concern with the problem of drawing out the potential artist and of providing him with a stimulating educational climate and a chance to acquire a perfect technique prompted me to create the well-known Bauhaus School of Design in Germany. Its novel method of education in design has been widely misunderstood and misinterpreted. The present generation is inclined to think of it as a rigid stylistic dogma of yesterday whose usefulness has come to an end because its ideological and technical premises are now outdated. This view confuses a method of approach with the practical results obtained by it at a particular period of its application. The Bauhaus was not concerned with the formulation of timebound, stylistic concepts, and its technical methods were not ends in themselves. *It was created to show how a multitude of individuals, willing to work concertedly but without losing their identity, could evolve a kinship of expression in their response to the challenges of the day.* Its aim was to give a basic demonstration of how to maintain *unity in diversity,* and it did this with the materials, techniques, and form concepts germane to its time. It was this method of approach that was revolutionary, and I have not found any new system of education for design which puts the Bauhaus idea out of course. In fact, the present disenchantment with the doubtful results obtained from simply imitating highly personal design methods of this or that master without adding to their substance should give renewed emphasis to the Bauhaus principles.

It would be most desirable if the initial work done by the Bauhaus were continued and expanded so that we would be able to draw on an ever-increasing common fund of objective knowledge, teachable to all age groups and furnishing the much needed vocabulary with which individuals are free to compose their personal design poetry. If the capacity to focus and crystallize the tendencies of a period becomes dim, as it has in our time, the necessity of intensifying our efforts at coherence becomes ever-more important. There are some vital centers in this country where such work is pursued with dedication, but their influence is still limited, and it is hard to find creative architects and artists who want to take on teaching positions besides their other work, because public opinion regards teaching as a mere backwater compared to the excitement and rewards of practical work. That the two must be combined if a healthy climate for the growing generation is to evolve remains an applauded theory rather than an actual accomplishment.

I remember an experience I had myself years ago when, on the occasion of my seventieth birthday, *Time* magazine commented on my career. After coming to this country, they said, I had been "content to teach only," as if this were, in itself, a minor occupation as compared to that of a practicing architect. Apart from the fact that the magazine was misinformed—I had never given up my practice—it brought home to me again the realization that the profession of the teacher is looked upon in this country as a kind of refuge for those visionaries who cannot hold their own in the world of action and reality. Though, admittedly, there has been a shift in this view lately, it is still much too firmly established to become uprooted overnight. It remains a tremendous handicap for those who realize the importance of combining practice and teaching and want to make their contribution in both fields.

What, now, can be done by the individual practicing architect to promote a greater measure of cooperation between those groups who contribute to the development of our visible world? In spite of our partiality to "togetherness," this fashionable trend has accomplished little in our field since it lacks a distinct purpose, a discipline, a working method of its own. All these must be found before we become more and more lost to each other.

I think we all agree that a relatedness of expression and a consolidation of trends cannot be consciously organized in a democracy, but springs from spontaneous group consciousness, from collective intuition, which brings our pragmatic requests and our spiritual desires into interplay. I have tried, for a long time, therefore, to give more incentive to such a state of mind by developing a spirit of voluntary teamwork among groups of architects. But my idea has become almost suspect since so many of my colleagues are still wedded to the nineteenth century idea that individual genius can only work in splendid isolation. Just as our profession fifty years ago closed its eyes to the fact that the machine had irrefutably entered the building process, so now it is trying to cling to the conception of the architect as a self-sufficient, independent operator, who, with the help of a good staff and competent engineers, can solve any problem and can in this way—and only in this way—keep his artistic integrity intact. This, in my view, is an isolationist attitude which will be unable to stem the tide of uncontrolled disorder engulfing our living spaces. It runs counter to the concept of "total architecture," which is concerned with the whole of our environmental development and demands collaboration on the broadest basis. Our present disparate way of solving problems of collaboration on large projects is simply to throw a few prominent architects together in the hope that five people will automatically produce more beauty than one. The result, as often as not, becomes an unrelated assemblage of individual architectural ideas, not an integrated whole of new and enriched value. It is obvious that we have to learn new and better ways of collaboration.

In my experience these methods call first of all for an unprejudiced state of mind and for the firm belief that common thought and action are a precondition for cultural growth. Starting on this basis, we must strive to acquire the methods, the vocabulary, the habits of collaboration with which most architects are unfamiliar. This is not easy to accomplish. It is one thing to condition an individual for cooperation by making him conform; it is another, altogether, to make him keep his identity within a group of equals while he is trying to find common ground with them. It is imperative, though, that we develop such a technique of collaboration to a high degree of refinement, since it is our guarantee for the protection of the individual against becoming a mere number and, at the same time, for the development of related expression rather than of pretentious individualism.

There can be no doubt, of course, that the creative spark originates always with the individual, but while he works in close cooperation with others and is exposed to their stimulating and challenging criticism, his own work matures more rapidly and never loses touch with the broader aspects which unite a team in a common effort.

Communication from person to person is at an all-time low today in spite of, or because of, our tremendous technical means of communication. Most individuals are driven into shallow superficiality in all their relations with other people, including their own friends. But just as the airplane is no substitute for our legs, so personal contact between people of like interests cannot be replaced by the vast output of professional literature and information services, because individual interpretation and exchange are still essential for our functioning as human beings. Our overextended receptive faculties need a respite so that greater concentration and intensification can take place; and I feel that a well-balanced team can help achieve just that. As we cannot inform ourselves simultaneously in all directions, a member of a team benefits from the different interests and attitudes of the other members during their collaborative meetings. The technical, social, and economic data, gathered individually and then presented to the others, reach them already humanized by personal interpretation, and, since all members of a team are apt to add their own different reactions, the new information is more easily seen in its proper perspective and its potential value.

For the effectiveness of this kind of intimate teamwork, two preconditions are paramount: voluntariness, based on mutual respect and liking, and exercise of individual leadership and responsibility within the group. Without the former, collaboration is mere expediency, and without the latter, it loses artistic integrity. To safeguard design coherence and impact, the right of making final decisions must therefore be left exclusively to the one member who happens to be responsible for a specific job, even though his decision should run counter to the opinion of other members.

Such principles of teamwork are easier explained than carried into practice because we all still arrive on the scene with our old habits of trying to beat the other fellow to it. But I believe that a group of architects willing to give collaboration a chance will be rewarded by seeing their effectiveness strengthened and their influence on public opinion broadened. All teams so organized, I trust, will eventually act as ferments in our drive for cultural integration.

Considering the reservoir of rich talent and the wealth of technical and financial resources available today, it would seem that this generation holds all the aces in the age-old game of creating new form symbols for the ideas by which a society lives. Only a magic catalyst seems to be needed to combine these forces and free them from isolation. I personally see this catalyst in the power of education—education to raise the expectations and demands a people make on their own form of living, education to waken and sharpen their latent capacities for creation and for cooperation. Creativity of the makers needs the response of all the users. I am convinced that a surprising amount of individual whimsy, yes, even aberration and downright ugliness, could be tolerated without causing serious harm if only the grand total design, the image a society should have of itself, would emerge clearly and unequivocally. What we admire in the achievements of successful city builders in former periods is the fact that their work reveals so clearly the ultimate destination to which each individual feature was put in as an organic part of the whole area. This was what made the city perform its functions well and gave the people a stimulating background for all their activities. How else can the marvel of the Piazza San Marco, this arch example of perfection, be explained? Not the work of a single master like the Piazza San Peter; we find, instead, that over a long period of growth a perfect balance was developed among the contributions of a number of architects, using many different materials and methods. They achieved this miracle because they never violated the main purpose of the general plan, yet never forced uniformity of design. San Marco is an ideal illustration to my credo *unity in diversity,* to the development of which, in our time, I can only hope to have made my personal contribution during a long life of search and discovery.

A New Pact
with Life

Address given at eightieth
birthday party, Cambridge,
Mass., May, 1963

11. Model of central section of Britz-Buckow-Rudow, Berlin. (See plan, p. 63.) Walter Gropius and Alexander Cvijanovic (The Architects Collaborative).
Photo: Robert D. Harvey, Boston, Mass.

A New Pact
with Life

In spite of all the lip service paid to it, there is still hardly a beginning at cooperation among *groups* of architects who, by choice or happenstance, are required to work side by side on larger projects. In all my recent experience, I have continually run into the same situation: a naïve disregard for what happens beyond the borderline of one's own commission, even among well-known architects. Whether you look at our newly built airports or universities, nowhere do we find expressed a conscious sense of coresponsibility for the unity of the whole plan, in spite of the participation of our most prominent architects. Neither has the client's attention been drawn to this important issue by the architects themselves, nor have they taken the initiative to sit down together to voluntarily agree on a set of proposals and limitations of what should be permissible under a given program

12. Housing project Britz-Buckow-Rudow, Berlin, 1960. Walter Gropius and Benjamin Thompson (The Architects Collaborative). Site plan. Apartments for 45,000 people. A central greenbelt with subway swings from northwest to east, crossed by radially running streets. Shopping centers at main crossroads.
Photo: Robert D. Harvey, Boston, Mass.

and finally to elect a coordinator among themselves charged with the responsibility of seeing that everybody abides by their joint decisions. The desire to outdistance everybody else in dramatic appeal is still so irresistible that the necessary balance of the total design is destroyed. This infringement on the architectural hierarchy, which, in a civilized society, should be self-regulating in accordance with the importance and purpose of the various buildings, is an asocial act, a cultural offense. I do not believe that an architect can exonerate himself from responsibility in this respect by asserting that he has not been put into this world to remake humanity and that he can do little but comply when he is asked by an uninhibited or ignorant client to disregard all else. I certainly do not underestimate the tremendous difficulties of this battle. In fact, I am involved at this point in one myself, and I feel the effects of it very keenly. I was commissioned together with TAC to design the master plan for a large development which will give 45,000 people a new living space. I am very much concerned, naturally, that the ideas and principles which have guided me and my partners in the conception of this plan should be kept intact throughout the whole procedure. A group of architects was chosen to submit housing designs for the different sectors of the development. They were asked to keep to the guiding principles upon which we had all agreed. When I was invited later to come to look at their design proposals, I found to my consternation that every one of them had proceeded according to his own imagination without paying any attention to the adjacent schemes of his colleagues or, for that matter, to the overall requirements of the general plan. There were good projects among them, but they all exhibited the same characteristic: they were *unrelated* to each other. They did not fit at their seams. I expressed my concern about this outcome, but, as usual, there is tremendous pressure to get started, and it will take all our efforts to make a stand in the fight to save this project from becoming another jumble of unintegrated individual contributions.

I know that many agree with the principal desirability of such cooperation, but where was it actually made to happen? Judgment Day is not far off for this century. Shall we persist in chaoticism?

These days I often receive letters from friends and read reports in magazines by people who have traveled in the more remote places of the world where our kind of prosperity has not yet arrived to confuse everybody. The reaction of our well-fed, well-clad traveler, coming from the land of abundance is very often the same: silent envy and nostalgia for a way of life where the frame still fits the picture, where a behavior code still matches the actual conditions of daily existence, where ritual still exemplifies living faith. We know very well, of course, that life in these communities is actually full of hardships and drudgery, but we immediately become conscious of the one great advantage they have over us—their performance is still convincing. They know how to behave in a society governed by the iron rules of necessity and scarcity, and they have, long ago, developed a religious or philosophical framework for this type of life which gives them the license to operate their human enterprises within the strict limitations of an accepted system. We, on the other hand, having stepped out of this confining background into the land of abundance, free choice, and limitless feasibility, are not at all as happy and confident as might be expected, because our emotional life is still conditioned by our early commitment to the economic and cultural standards of the past. Many of us operate, so to speak, with a bad conscience and often even with a certain revulsion against this cornucopia that has been emptied over our heads. In short, we feel we have not yet received our license for living on this new scale, and a valid textbook of orientation is still missing. In many cases it is not even quite clear what is commendable and what is destructive for our society, and the architect and planner, who is supposed to create the physical structure for this vague situation, can only proceed from his personal convictions with no assurance that *his* will be the kind of contribution which will help modern man to make a new pact with life which he so badly needs. This is the great risk and adventure we all have to face, and there is no ultimate comfort in reverting to answers found for an earlier age.

This brings up the question of our attitude toward tradition. Tradition, seen from the architectural point of view, has of course always meant more to me than the easy imitation of the outward forms of past periods or past modes of life. It has meant capturing the real spirit of a certain region as it evolves through long interaction between the natural setting, the type of people who inhabit it, and the dominant spiritual and practical factors that determine their way of life. Ap-

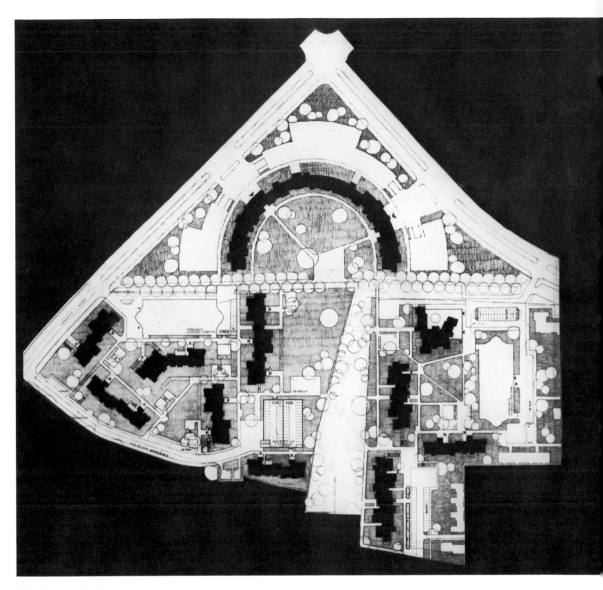

13. Site plan for the central section of
Britz-Buckow-Rudow. Designed for the development
corporations "Gehag," "Ideal," and "Hilfswerk"
by Walter Gropius and Alexander Cvijanovic (The
Architects Collaborative).
Photo: Robert D. Harvey, Boston, Mass.

proached in this way, any major shift in the production, techniques, and social order of such a region should find expression in its architecture so that the *living* issues can be read from its lines as well as those of the past.

The living issues. . . . Looking back into history it always seems that past periods were acutely conscious of what constituted their major concern, and only when we come down to our own period does it seem so fiendishly difficult to agree on what we would all consider to be our most important, common motives and aims. But unless we find out and bring material sacrifices in order to be able to demonstrate them clearly, we shall not understand ourselves, much less be understood by others.

In the recent past we have concerned ourselves more with defining ever-newer *means* than with defining *ends,* and we have amassed

14. Model of a highrise apartment block in Britz-Buckow-Rudow, Berlin. Walter Gropius and Alexander Cvijanovic (The Architects Collaborative). *Photo: Robert D. Harvey, Boston, Mass.*

such a tremendous arsenal of techniques that their bristling display has nearly robbed us of our sense of balance. Twenty-two years ago, when I first arrived in the United States, it was, for instance, still possible in Massachusetts to squelch an unusual proposal with the words, "It isn't done." This, of course, can be either a virtue or a handicap, depending on how it is used. It was an impasse which could not be overcome by clever argumentation, since its mainspring lay in certain agreements between people who had accepted a particular code of life and considered themselves bound by its unwritten rules.

No such code exists today; everything *can* be done and, most certainly, *is* being done. Our cities have taken on the look of a free-for-all; wild competition to engage the mind, heart, and body of its population, and all sense of propriety and discrimination seems to have been swept away by this unlimited technical dam burst. The old watchword "Let's put first things first" has lost its meaning since we seem unable to remember clearly *what should* come first. No visitor from Mars could possibly gain an understanding of our order of life by looking at our newest man-made world.

It is interesting in this respect to note that if the democratic societies have so far not shown enough unity of purpose to bring about convincing manifestations of general *cultural* significance, the authoritarian societies have contributed even less cultural coherence in this century. Ideas can apparently be instilled by an act of will and with the help of strong directional control, but they can never be made to flower into art by decree.

What ingredient, without which we cannot hope to emerge from visual chaos, is missing in our way of life? The answer has thrust itself upon us for a long time now, but we are still far from a general recognition of the fact that a society such as ours, which has conferred equal privileges on everybody, must acknowledge its duty to raise the general level of responsiveness to spiritual and aesthetic values by *education*. As it is, the individual is insufficiently trained to see and to observe that the visual phenomena around himself and his environment, in its present, chaotic state, does little to provide him with the realization that beauty is a basic requirement of life. It is this realization, though, that is a necessary precondition for organic building and planning.

The realization that only a broad educational attempt would eventually create the premises for a greater, cultural unity had caused me to establish, right after World War I, the Bauhaus in Germany and, when Germany reverted to the dictatorial methods I had hoped we had outgrown, to transfer my educational work to the Graduate School of Design at Harvard University.

In the meantime the Bauhaus idea has spread far and wide, but it also has been abused and distorted in such a manner that there is now a popular version of a fixed "Bauhaus Style" which is tossed around in debate as if it had really existed as a rigidly defined formula. On the contrary. Our strength was that there was no dogma, no prescription—things that invariably go stale after a while—but only a guiding hand and an immensely stimulating setting for those who were willing to work concertedly, but without losing their identities. What made our group function was a common method of approach, a kindred way of responding to challenges of our day, a similar *Weltanschauung,* if you will. We knew that only a personal interpretation of the common phenomena of life can become art, that only an individual searching mind can find a conceptual attitude and pose questions of principle; but we also knew that it was imperative simultaneously to find the bond of a common expression to achieve a balance between individual initiative and voluntary subordination to a common principle. Under these same principles, my partners and I are working in The Architects Collaborative.

One of the bequests of the nineteenth century which still handicaps us today is the obsession with the idea that individual genius can work only in exalted isolation, a view which was quite foreign to other periods. It prevents the public mind from understanding the new efforts at collaboration among architects and artists which characterize present development, and it constantly throws us back into unwarranted jealousies and confusions.

One of the fallacies of our present conception of life results, I believe, from the fact that a majority of people believe that the modern organization man has found today's version of that indispensable ingredient of all cultures—the intellectual common denominator of a period. He has not. For with his new tool, automation, he performs only one aim: to compel each individual to abide by a narrowly circumscribed intellectual code, the focus of which is mere expediency. Adaptability is rated higher by him than independent thought, and consequently the individual becomes lost within the group. Against this robotization of our society, we must set our conviction that keeping one's identity is *superior* to social usefulness at any price and that a *leveling* process can never produce a cultural common denominator.

But didn't we only yesterday run down the rugged individualist? We did, but the pendulum has swung back sharply to the other extreme now, and we have to discover the hard way that neither conformity within the group—which leads to tyranny by the majority—nor willful extravagance of the individual can create a climate which favors the development of initiative and imagination, but that it is the moral responsibility carried by each individual independently within the group which provides the basis for the goal of a democratic culture, i.e., *unity in diversity.*

We stand at a moment in history that calls for a bold, imaginative interpretation of the democratic idea. Our generation is presented with a similar challenge as were the founders of our Western culture, the Greeks, when they deliberately buried the treasures and temples of their former existence under the triumphant symbol of their newly found freedom: the Acropolis. Or, as Thornton Wilder has put it so beautifully: "Culture under a democracy has its dangers, but also its hopes and promises. Here a new and tremendous theme opens up which will have to be penetrated by thought, investigated and expressed; the theme: Man with head unbowed. Democracy has the new task to create new myths, new metaphors, new images to show forth the state of new dignity which man has entered upon." Only when a social or spiritual goal has thus become clearly identified in the mind of a society does it become the inner substance of its works of art and architecture.

Tradition and Continuity in Architicture

Address given at the Boston
Architectural Center,
February, 1964.
First published by *Architectural
Record,* May, June, July, 1964

Tradition and Continuity
in Architecture

There is no past which we should long to resurrect,
There is eternal newness only, reconstituting itself
Out of the extended elements of the past
And true yearning should always be towards productive ends
Making some new, some better thing.

Goethe

Looking at our state of democracy today, we realize that improvement of our society can come only from a greater effort to educate ever-stronger independent individuals who will be capable of developing, simultaneously, a group consciousness among them. From such group consciousness—as history shows—develops tradition and continuity. The more outspoken the individuals of a society are, and the more they are willing at the same time to abide by commonly recognized group characteristics, the stronger will be their cultural manifestations. No doubt, length and depth of the historical development of a people are reason for the greater or lesser stability of their tradition. The United States, the famous melting pot of so many races and nations, is still in a state of fermentation. Small wonder then that no consistency of approach is yet noticeable in modern American architec-

15. St. Thomas, New York, neogothic church, and a skyscraper on Fifth Ave. Violation of hierarchy. The cultural building within the urban fabric needs to be emphasized by setting it off from neighboring buildings. Here it is overpowered by a commercial giant.

71

ture. In fact, we grope in many directions to find our own. Cultural group consciousness is not yet strongly in evidence. Since the history of our civilization is still young, this is quite natural, and we had better admit that the visual documentation of our specific way of life is still largely haphazard and inconclusive.

How can we bring the diverging lines of development into better focus so that our hands become firmer in drawing the outlines of a recognizable image of our society as it reveals itself in its buildings and planning habits? How can we assess our own contributions in the light of traditional values and the idea of continuity in a cultural sense?

Ever since we have placed ourselves on the fast-moving vehicle of scientific progress, we have only allowed our minds to be dragged along by it at an ever-increasing speed, while our souls got off at an early stage, hurling loud protests after the "infernal machine." How are we going to join our parted selves again and balance the impact of the vehicle? Certainly not by embellishing the scene of havoc afterwards with architectural "gems" which, by eclectic overtones, strive to create a link with an emotionally meaningful past. It isn't that easy.

When I came to this country in 1937, I found a naïve but confident belief among the average people that everything new was better than everything old. This belief has undergone a considerable disillusion in the meantime, and lately, some arbiters of "taste" have let it be known that almost anything old is preferable to anything new. The free-roaming spirit of adventure has curled in on itself. This is where we stand now, our hands uncertain because our minds are; with diminished confidence because our conscience tells us that we have not fully played our part in the great task of this century: the transformation of the inarticulate, drifting masses of democratic citizens into individuals aware of their own potentialities and responsibilities. Accusing the general public of cultural inaction will only retard the recognition of the deeper cause for our frustration: our hesitation to stand up heart and soul for the tasks this century has imposed on us and to see them through to a seemly end. Only this would be of historical relevance, and nobody is going to remember the half-hearted and the strays.

In the beginning of this century, architects were misguided into believing that their duty lay in disguising the raw facts of the new industrial, urban life that had sprung up around them and that they must guard the continuity of immutable aesthetic concepts as they had been developed by the centuries preceding them. They lost sight of the fact that this misapprehension of their role in society gradually reduced their activities to the well-to-do fringes of society where the preaching was easy and where their standing as elegant arbiters of taste was assured. I grew up in that atmosphere. When in 1910 I had my first premonition that all this would be wholly inadequate to establish a true, historically valid expression of the needs of our own time, I felt strongly that it would be necessary for the architectural profession to throw itself fully into the creation of an architect-controlled production of all the innumerable building facets which combine to make up the setting for the whole of twentieth-century society. At the same time, I felt it should revolutionize the visual education of the young.

In the pursuit of these aims I bloodied my nose repeatedly in my attempts, first, to give prefabrication for the mass market an early, architect-controlled start and, second, to put visual education on a much broader and more contemporary basis as we finally succeeded in doing at the Bauhaus. These efforts I continued in different countries and on different levels; but among professional ranks there was scant sympathy for this early effort at giving direction to the ominously gathering forces of mass production before they were going to swamp us. The sight of the straitjacket into which architects proceeded to maneuver themselves had already worried me and other architects before World War I, but, as you know, the majority of them continued at that time to confine themselves to the limited demands of the decorator's craft; and today, fifty years later, prefabrication is still largely unattended by architects, and visual training is far from being on an equal level with other subjects of education.

But despite this poor record in foresight and anticipation of an inevitable development, architects never hesitate to berate the dastardly citizen for his ignorance in matters of architectural design. This again became a matter of public record recently when the shameful handling of the taxation of the Seagram building—which amounts to a penalty being paid for excellence in design and good craftsmanship—was discussed. This bad decision should indeed be protested, but it seems too easy to accuse the general insensitivity of an anonymous culprit, the city officials, the courts, or the unenlightened businessmen, when architects must really share the blame for these shortcomings together with all those others who failed to read the signs of the times. If we had pressed long ago for a more profound visual training of the average school child, who, though born with the ability to *see*, must be trained to develop his ability to *perceive;* if we had been fully alert to the changing demands of the times, we might be nearer to a meeting of the minds when we have to map out a general strategy for the appearance of our common habitat nowadays.

Have architects learned from this defeat? Not too eagerly. In fact they are beginning to become susceptible again to the exhortations of those devoted advocates of the past who acknowledge the present only when softened by accents of some romantic disguise or other to give it the appearance of legitimacy. The word "tradition" is bandied around again for the superficial purpose of ennobling this or that piece of "mood architecture" and to construe facile "links with the past" for the half educated.

The word "tradition" comes from the Latin: *tradere,* i.e., transmit, carry on. This certainly does not mean that the study of an old, successful house type or an old, successful town structure would necessarily equip one to construct a house or city fit for *this* century; in fact, too-deep absorption in it might hinder instead of help an immediate and fresh response to our modern problems. What we *should* gain from such studies is an admiration for the direct, unsentimental, and exuberant solutions which have been found in the past, not necessarily by famous architects only, but by ordinary people who obeyed necessity in an inspired way because they identified themselves wholeheartedly with their own times. This group instinct, as I have said before, is by no means fully developed in this country, and the influence some of our intellectuals have had does little to knit individuals together for a common effort. Highly cultivated themselves, in esoteric *apartheid,* they let the realities of our contemporary scene enter their lives only in the safe, symbolic form of modern painting and sculpture. By creating islands of culture for themselves in putting up museum buildings and other tokens of civilization in the midst of otherwise shapeless hodgepodge towns, they make themselves believe that they

16. Grand Central City Building (Pan Am),
New York, 1963. Walter Gropius with The
Architects Collaborative, Pietro Belluschi,
and Emery Roth and Sons. The fifty-nine-story
building straddling Park Ave. creates a new
focus for this sector of the city.
Photo: Joseph W. Molitor, Ossining, N.Y.

have done their part in carrying the cultural message among the un-enlightened. But they carefully stay away from those areas where the actual face of our time reveals itself in its depressing ugliness, and they do not share in the labors of those who are trying, at this late date, to develop a new blueprint for living for the multitudes who have been vainly waiting to see an image of their own society arise in which they can believe. So, by and large, the cultural message is lost to the inhabitants of Shantytown.

No doubt the visual illiteracy and helplessness, which have become characteristic of the average citizen of industrialized countries the world over, are a formidable handicap for the architect of today and one which can be overcome only by patient, long-term educational influence. To arrive at established standards of evaluation is the slowly accruing result of long efforts, made over generations, which have made people responsive and sensitive to the meaning of form and its symbolic powers. During the speedy changeover of our civilization from a locally centered, nationally bound system of values to the free-moving world exchange of experience, research, and material goods, our former values have become obscured, and the new insights have not yet found the voluntary general acceptance which would be needed to make them effective. One outcome of this disorientation is the present habit of seeing art and architecture as mere luxury or status symbols, while it formerly was the deeply rooted, un-self-conscious imagery of people who shared a common code and who could be sure of response when any one of them raised his voice or hand in creative work.

In our pathetic rush for at least token participation in the new world of kaleidoscopic patterns and schemes which has enveloped us, we have forced certain sectors of the human mind into accelerated development while others remain locked in their traditional attitudes. The slowness in correlating our highly developed powers of intellectual reasoning with our half-hidden emotional impulses has produced a deep cleavage in the minds of men. This splitting up of one's life into separate segments, unconnected by the driving force of a central conviction, destroys coherence and unity, so evident in our urban environment. We seem to have lost control temporarily, and continuity

17. John F. Kennedy
Federal Office Building,
Boston, Mass., 1964. Walter
Gropius and Norman C.
Fletcher (The Architects
Collaborative) and Samuel
Glaser Associates.
Photo: Peter Holmes

18. Reston, Va. Airview. Imaginative solution
for a modern township. Pleasant alternation
of building heights.
Photo: Stan Wayman, Life.

in a cultural sense seems threatened. Only the determination and courage to live up to our own insights consistently, to practice what we profess, to draw together what threatens to slip apart, and to pick up the live thread instead of the dead one can help us propel tradition and continuity forward into the future.

You know that I, for my part, have always been identified since the early twenties with the idea of "functionalism" as the only straight and narrow line to take us into this future. But in the interpretation of those with only sectorially developed minds, this line has become indeed so straight and narrow that, for them, it led straight to a dead end. Its original complexity and psychological implications, as we developed them in the Bauhaus, were forgotten, and it was decried as a simple-minded, purely utilitarian approach to design, devoid of any imagination that would give grace and beauty to life. To this I can only say that the revolution of the twenties was total and moral, and its creators looked at beauty not as something self-consciously "added on," but as something that was believed to be inherent in the vitality, appropriateness, and psychological significance of a designed object, whether it was a building, a piece of furniture, or a stage design. We

19. Bath, England. The Royal Crescent. Famed one-family town houses. Urban order without monotony.

knew and taught that space relations, proportions, and colors control psychological functions which are as vital and real as any performance data for structural or mechanical parts and for the use value of a plan. If our early attempts looked somewhat stark and sparse, it is because we had just found a new vocabulary with which to speak out, and this we wanted to set in the greatest possible contrast to the overstuffed bombast that had gone before. Besides, we were often held down to a minimum of expenditure by a public which could only

20. Levittown, N.Y., 1958. Accumulation of monotonously strung-out family houses. No organic layout nor communal facilities. The individual becomes a mere number.
Photo: Life.

be sold on modern architecture when it promised to be cheaper; its aesthetic possibilities were not even suspected.

As the evolution of form develops always in successive waves of reactions against preceding trends, it is only natural that these early testimonies to a newly found freedom in architectural design have been followed by a wealth of new conceptions and refinements in the field of space relations and in the use of new techniques. If one compares the typical architecture of the twenties with that of today, the most significant development lies in the increasing accentuation of three-dimensional plasticity. Structural boniness, curved shells, recessed and protruding building parts offer a rich play of light and shadow absent from the flat surfaces of the curtain wall which, for so long, had become the one-sided trademark of modern architecture. Personal interpretations of these fresh experiences have enriched our vocabulary and pleased our audience, and the stage seems to be set for a major contribution to the evolving image of our time—if we could only keep from straying into a new eclecticism or from adopting a sort of super-functionalism that borders on mysticism. Curiously, nothing seems harder to achieve right now than a sober, straightforward, balanced approach which would allow us to solve our design problems without bending over backward too far in our desire to include all possible tricks of a scholarly or a technical nature which are at our disposal today.

These defects, which weaken our hand, are partly a reflection of the vain efforts of the average citizen to seek an emotional affinity with the past which, in practice, he is unwittingly denying with his every action. Whether the dishonest label "ranch house" is put on a mass-produced little commodity, or whether "home laid eggs" are sold to a nostalgic customer, it all plays up to his longing to be comforted by familiar phrases, at least, if not by familiar sights.

Our very real need to develop an understanding for historical continuity is not helped by these flights into make-believe, but these do not only occur at the commercial level; even our best minds succumb sometimes to the urge of galvanizing remnants of the past into an artificial participation in the activities of the present. The problem of what to protect and what to destroy haunts all cities with a proud past. Significant and venerable landmarks should, of course, be incorporated into the growing city pattern as far as possible. Nobody will want to miss, for instance, the old cemetery on busy Tremont Street in Boston. There are some cities, like Rome, for example, that have been remarkably successful in their attempts to preserve the old and even the ancient sections of town in unadulterated fashion, but this can usually be accomplished only in places where the resulting loss in productivity and livability can be offset by their income-producing value as tourist attractions. Without the tourists gazing at its wonders and using them as a backdrop to all kinds of entertainment, the city of Venice—to name only one—would be hard put to make a decent living in its present setting. As for less famous sites and buildings, it becomes more and more difficult to maintain, along with the old structures, the specific atmosphere which created them in the first place and without which they seem unanimated. The concern for preservation per se should not mislead us into creating lifeless islands—museums—which cannot be assimilated by the life of the city. There is no *one* answer to the solution of these problems, and each case must be treated on its own merits.

The majority of American cities are less often confronted with these dilemmas than the old European and Asian ones. But the uproar about the changes that have occurred on Park Avenue in New York shows that here also the citizen hates to part with familiar sights on the one hand, though, on the other, he precipitates their disappearance in all manners and ways at his disposal. *The proposal to freeze certain aesthetically pleasant town patterns, which have outlived their compelling usefulness for the actual life that goes on in them, into a memorial for a former social setup, will always come to grief if the citizen no longer shares the tenets which made this particular setup possible.* Much as he may like the looks of it from long association, he will inevitably destroy it by letting the tools which accommodate his own way of life sweep in, be it in the form of vehicles or buildings. If the citizens of Manhattan had been really serious about wanting to save Park Avenue's spacious, dignified former appearance, they should have protested when the very first skyscraper threatened to go up, because this event spelled the end of a well-worked-out system of order and proportion which had distinguished Park Avenue from other thoroughfares.

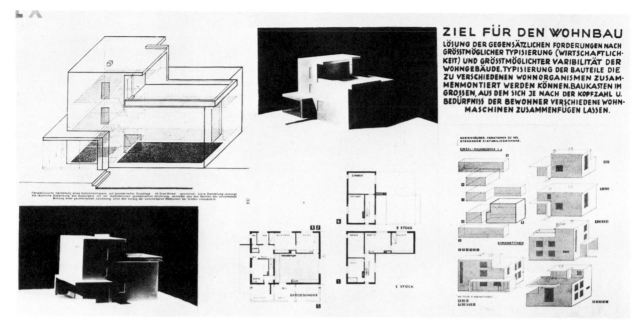

ZIEL FÜR DEN WOHNBAU

LÖSUNG DER GEGENSÄTZLICHEN FORDERUNGEN NACH GRÖSSTMÖGLICHER TYPISIERUNG (WIRTSCHAFTLICHKEIT) UND GRÖSSTMÖGLICHTER VARIBILITÄT DER WOHNGEBÄUDE. TYPISIERUNG DER BAUTEILE DIE ZU VERSCHIEDENEN WOHNORGANISMEN ZUSAMMENMONTIERT WERDEN KÖNNEN. BAUKASTEN IM GROSSEN, AUS DEM SICH JE NACH DER KOPFZAHL U. BEDÜRFNISS DER BEWOHNER VERSCHIEDENE WOHNMASCHINEN ZUSAMMENFÜGEN LASSEN.

21. Standardized building segments. Walter Gropius, 1923. Proposal for standard types of housing, combining opposite demands: Greatest possible variation with greatest possible standardization.

22. Standardized building elements. Models. Walter Gropius, 1923. Possibility of variation though repeating identical building elements.

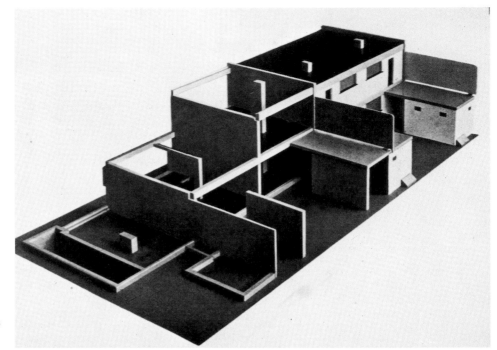

23. Housing project
Dessau-Törten.
Walter Gropius, 1928.
Prefabricated row houses,
developed for the "Reichs
Research Institute for
Economy in Housing."

25. One-family house for Werkbund
Exhibition, Stuttgart. Walter Gropius,
1927. Assembly from prefabricated parts.
Photo: Dr. Lossen.

4. Housing project Dessau-Törten. Walter Gropius, 1928.
odel of the structural system of row houses.

26. Prefabricated copper house. Walter Gropius, 1931. Variety resulting from different combinations of standardized parts. Wood frame, insulated with aluminum foils and sheathed with corrugated copper sheets outside and eternit (asbestos) inside.

27. Plan of expansible, prefabricated one-family house. Walter Gropius, 1943. Developed in collaboration with Konrad Wachsmann for the "General Panel Corporation."

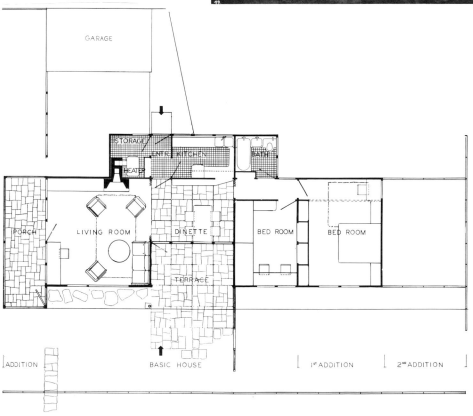

28. Prefabricated house for the "General Panel
Corporation." Walter Gropius and Konrad Wachsmann,
1943–1945. The method of prefabrication was
developed for a module of 3'-4" = 1 meter.
Photo: Anna Wachsmann.

It was a break in continuity and tradition when the city of New York neglected to replace the old zoning law by a new one which would similarly impose a unifying height limit and building line for all buildings on this street, but now geared to the new order of magnitude which was imposed on this part of the city by the gradual transformation of its former functions to its present one as a business and trade center. The failure to act properly at this strategic moment has sanctioned a commercial development in an uncontrolled free-for-all spirit on the avenue, and unless we want to challenge the very idea of the free enterprise policy, with its vested interest in the property value of land, it becomes pure hypocrisy to cry wolf now when free enterprise asserts itself. It is inconceivable that it should be expected to refrain from using its privileges and assume instead a noble attitude of financial sacrifice when nothing in our national book of conduct taught it so. It is futile and self-deceiving to expect from this, our system of expediency, more than an occasional gesture toward better town planning at the present time. Once it should become generally apparent that good business is not necessarily identical with good living, this attitude may become obsolete, but that time, unfortunately, has not yet arrived.

This story of the detrimental effect of city inaction shows that mere occupation with studies of the traditional past, as it is exercised today in our general education, obviously does not by itself secure responsible continuity and vigilance. I, myself, have often been accused of having withheld the teaching of art history from the Bauhaus students and to have insisted that such courses were relegated to the later years of studies at the Graduate School of Design in Harvard. I had my very good reasons for this, and they were certainly not the outcome of a presumptuous disregard for the grand achievements of former periods.

With regard to the students of the Bauhaus, who had just emerged from a long period of frustration with a frozen status quo, the introduction of regular art history courses would have caused an instant emotional defiance. It seemed to be a much more urgent task at that time to release the pent-up creative energies that had been suppressed for generations.

With regard to the Harvard curriculum, I acted upon the experience my own development had taught me: that the study of art history, imposed at a time when the student is filled with his own thoughts and works and has not yet felt a genuine curiosity for the works of the past, remains unassimilated, dead knowledge. There had been times when I had shut myself off for years from any studies of the past, only to resume them happily and with better judgment and appreciation later on when I felt firmer ground under my own feet and became more articulate in my own thinking and doing. A new insight, a sudden recognition, may be triggered into consciousness by incidental or planned confrontation with a masterwork of the past, and from there on it is not a guilty conscience, but keenest sympathy, which keeps an individual voluntarily on the track of history, and nobody needs to worry any more about how much he will absorb. At this point, an inspired teacher may be able to open up new worlds of visual experience to him and to deepen his understanding for the underlying conditioning factors that shaped the image of this or that period. If he can awaken a student to the infinite possibilities of visual creativity and to the need to extend his own responsibilities beyond the immediate concerns into the larger context of past and future, he will have added a new dimension to the student's personal insights and aspirations. But this enriching experience should come only after he has already weathered his own first encounters with the practical process of design. Nothing increases respect and admiration for the masterpieces of the past more than having been face-to-face with one's own inadequacies in solving even a simple task of planning and constructing. When confronted too early with the great works of architectural history, a sensitive beginner may be rather more intimidated than stimulated, and, since, in my view, nothing must ever endanger his developing a creative approach to design right at the start, the studies of art history, I believe, should not be placed at the beginning of the curriculum. They should be put into the later years of training when time must be found to broaden his knowledge in the humanities, to make him into a well-rounded, well-educated personality.

Eventually, though, it is only the positive involvement with the forces that shape our *own* time which will generate that identity of belief and action which is so indispensable for a new cultural effort. Sureness and experience come from being exposed to the realities of *present* living and doing, not from sentiment, nor from seeing Pompeii. Those who are endowed with genuine creative talent and who have been taught the age-old obligation of the architect to relate his personal contribution meaningfully to the general aspect of the environment will almost instinctively achieve a successful coexistence of the new with the old, while the uncreative mind will produce stillborn solutions however much he has devoted himself to the study of art history.

Only that type of society takes up the thread of tradition in earnest which has educated itself to convey its own image via a specific visual order, well secured by a self-imposed ethical code. It is this moral force which embodies its quality of permanence while its ever-changing features replace each other in unending continuity. They are only temporary answers, from one time-limited conception to the other, intuitively taken out of the immense reservoir of the unknown and then consciously articulated by ever-growing knowledge.

This deepening and consolidating of a newly grasped truth, which helps build true tradition, is too often missing in the turbulence of our times. Magazines and newspapers have favored a publicity which applauds the stunnning surprise effect of architecture over the patient and consistent search for fundamental solutions, capable of development, growth, and repetition. I quote here Sir Christopher Wren who said, "Variety of uniformities makes complete beauty." We, however, have become top-heavy with personal contributions of a more-or-less glamorous nature which then *fail* to find their necessary foil in a dignified, restrained background architecture of a rather impersonal, collective character. The building of extraordinary character and importance *needs* such a background to function well in a visual sense. The love and care which other periods have lavished on these more anonymous prototypes of a public spirit of decency and propriety can be admired to this day in the famous street patterns of the Rue Rivoli in Paris or Beacon Street in Boston or the brownstone houses in New York. In our own time, architects have left these "grey" areas largely to the commercial builder to fill up, or they have introduced such a confusing variety of shapes and techniques in one and the same building area that their different structures never attained a common rhythm and close relationship. The modern urge for personal glorification has warped our standards and confused our goals.

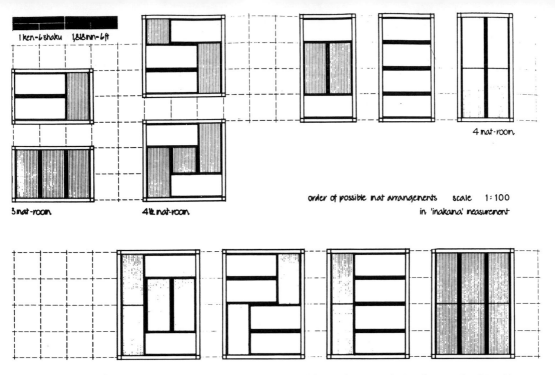

1 ken=6 shaku 1,818 mm=6 ft

order of possible mat arrangements   scale   1:100
in 'inakana' measurement

3 mat-room   4½ mat-room   4 mat-room

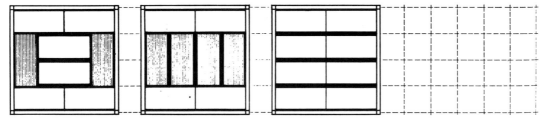

the hatching of certain mats indicates the different light values of mat texture according to light incidence, examples show light source from left or right

8 mat-room

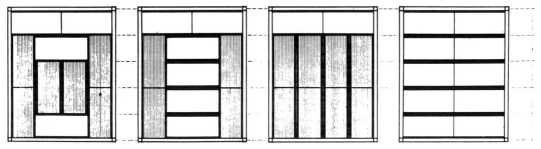

10 mat-room

29. Japanese square measure for dwellings.
The standard size of a Tatami mat is about
1 meter × 2 meters (3'-4" × 6'-8").
From: Engel, "The Japanese House."

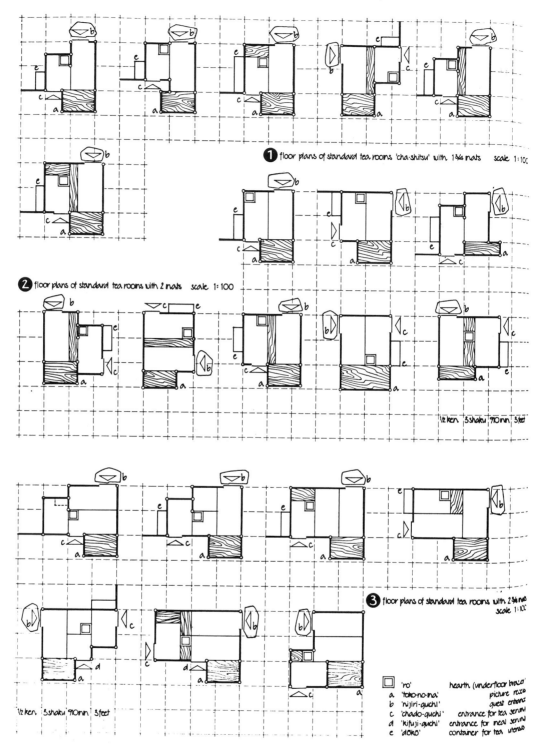

① floor plans of standard tea rooms 'cha-shitsu' with 1¾ mats   scale 1:100

② floor plans of standard tea rooms with 2 mats   scale 1:100

½ ken   3 shaku   910mm   3 feet

③ floor plans of standard tea rooms with 2¾ mats
scale 1:100

½ ken   3 shaku   910mm   3 feet

□	'ro'	hearth (underfloor brazier)
a	'toko-no-ma'	picture recess
b	'nijiri-guchi'	guest entrance
c	'chado-guchi'	entrance for tea serving
d	'kifuji-guchi'	entrance for meal serving
e	'doko'	container for tea utensils

30. The Japanese Tatami mat. This illustrates the varying Tatami patterns in teahouses.
From: Engel, "The Japanese House."

How else can we explain, for instance, the indifference with which the architectural profession has looked on one of the true means of coping with this problem: that of prefabrication? For fear that the introduction of prefabrication would impair their commitment to individual expression, the majority of architects bypassed its development almost completely, only to be rewarded finally by the ugly sight of shoddy, commercial minimum housing creeping all over the countryside. We have almost lost *that* battle, but we are in danger of losing more, unless we learn to speak up more forcefully on the cardinal problem facing every planner of our environment: the obstruction to sound development caused by private ownership of land. Though our deeply rooted belief in the sacred right of private property is undergoing a certain mutation, the process of legalizing a growing awareness that the right of the people must supersede the right of the individual has made little progress in the face of powerful opposition. A beginning of a solution has been established by the public right of expropriation, which, however, is only rarely applied forcefully enough though common interests are at stake. It is obvious that, particularly for a broad and farsighted renewal of urban areas, collective ownership of the land is a necessary precondition. Eventually rentability of land for a lifetime or for limited periods may replace outright individual ownership.

In the struggle for more effective urbanistic planning and design, which would restore a sense of identity and balance to the total fabric of a city or a region, we must strengthen the fading image of the architect as a man who helps his community achieve these aims. It isn't enough for him to be rushing on stage with a fancy proposal that promises nothing so much as to be a monument to his own ego.

When we skim today's magazines, we find too little attention paid to the virtues of restraint and much too little consideration given to the effect the addition of a new building has on the overall picture of a certain location. The observance of a definite hierarchy of buildings in their urban placement, their accessibility, and their more or less lavish treatment was exercised formerly by compulsion and order, coming usually from a central governing power. Unless we can replace this autocratic means of creating order out of chaos by voluntary action of an educated public, we shall never be able to

31. Flexible prototype elementary school
(The Architects Collaborative, 1954).
System building.

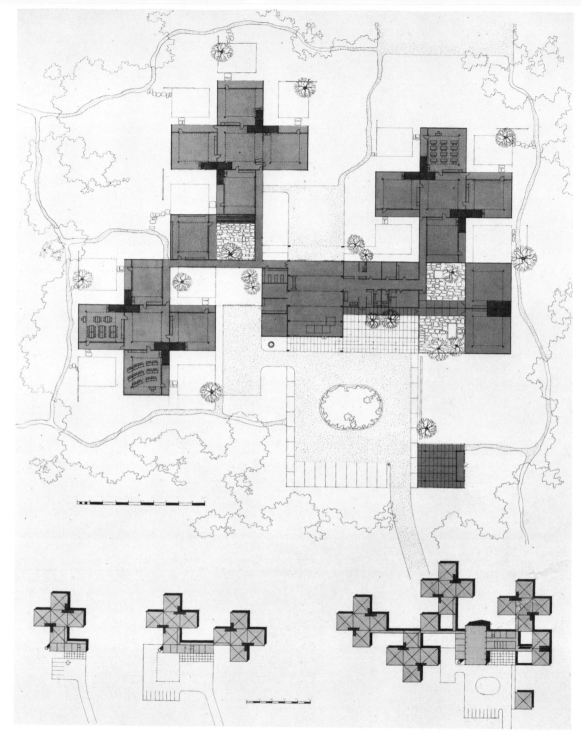

32. Various cluster positions of classroom
units (The Architects Collaborative). Basic unit
of the school, adaptable to any type of site,
is a cross composed of four classrooms
around a central multipurpose room.

follow up the city patterns of former times with an equally impressive and convincing one of the twentieth century. Are we fearful of losing our cherished individual identity as architects if we abide by an agreed-upon common code for the development of a certain district? Is our sense for the orchestral quality of city planning so poorly developed that we constantly give in to the temptation of displaying ourselves as brilliant soloists, even when the situation calls for the production of the kind of carefully composed but undemonstrative civic architecture which is destined to become the connective tissue of a whole urban area?

Past periods have striven wholeheartedly and by elaborate means to arrive at typical solutions for man's dwelling which managed to represent a ubiquitous and proud image of the prevailing character of

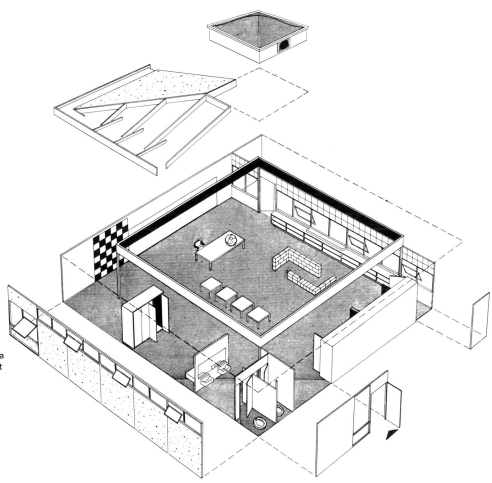

33. Isometric representation of a single classroom. Roof and front walls are drawn detached.

their society. Why do we submit to being outdelivered and outfigured by commercial developers who answer a crying public need for shelter by providing monotonous stretches of repetitious housing without any organic neighborhood composition? In spite of all the technical means at our disposal and the know-how to apply them, architects have been guilty of furthering the public misapprehension that prefabrication in the housing field would reduce the individual owner to a mere number in the general esteem. By derision and nonparticipation in this field, they have actively helped to bring about the fake individualistic housing which now disgraces most newly opened tracts of land. Genuine variety without monotony could have been attained if we had taken greater interest and influence in the development and design of an ever more comprehensive production of standardized, component building *parts* which could be assembled into a wide diversity of house types. Instead the idea of prefabrication was seized by manufacturing firms who came up with the stifling project of mass producing whole house types instead of component parts only. The resulting monotony further deepened the horror of a nostalgic, sentimental, unguided public of a prefabricated future. Now, when prefabrication has almost wholly conquered the manufacturing of the construction parts of skyscrapers, we find ourselves still in kindergarten with respect to its application in the housing industry.

To really make a success of it, the infinite component parts of houses must be separately prefabricated and then assembled into units which differ in size and appearance according to the needs and wishes of individual families. Starting with normed dimensions, equally fitting parts can be manufactured in competition on the free market, resulting in a great variety of machine-made component parts at the disposal of architects and their clients. This method of approach, which I have proposed since 1910, still stands, I believe. Instead of the wild riot of uncontrolled forms and colors of individual houses competing with each other—which we are so well familiar with today —the emphasis would be redirected at the unification of a whole street to whose civilized, overall appearance every individual building would be subordinated without, however, losing its individual accents by different proportioning, detail, color, and relation to open space. Harmonious integration, not regimentation, is the architectural goal.

All the preconditions to proceed successfully and simultaneously to fulfill our traditional obligations are there. If we don't act, it is our mind which is at fault, not the state of our material achievements.

After I have watched the coming and going opportunities over half a century, I confess to be impatient with our inertia and the recent tendency to stand wailing at the grave of the nineteenth century. This belated pose is unbecoming and sterile, and youth should close their ears to wailers and weepers who fear that their sophisticated appetites will never be sufficiently titillated by a straightforward, unsentimental approach to our present building problems. Why, for instance, do we dissipate our strength by fighting battles for the resurrection or preservation of structures which were monuments to a particularly insignificant period in American architectural history, a period which, still unsure of its own mission, threw the Roman toga around its limbs to appease its nagging doubts and thereby created what I call a "slipcover civilization"? Pennsylvania Station in New York is such a case of pseudotradition. True, its space conception shows a certain grandeur, commemorating the time when railways were the latest and most powerful means of opening up the American continent. But it must be remembered that it was built at a time when Frank Lloyd Wright had already made his powerful and unmistakably indigenous contribution to architecture. Pennsylvania Station, compared to this, was only a throwback to the empty mannerism inspired by the dependence of the American businessman on European prototypes of the so-called "ageless masterpieces." Today, of course, the spotlight of public attention has shifted from the railway gate to the jetport, and the building has become a liability instead of an asset. Time is an irresistible creator as well as destroyer of shapes and values. Single buildings, even as whole towns, have a life and death cycle similar to that of human beings and, within this cycle of constant change and renewal, it is our ethical standards and principles which are the enduring factors and should guide our decisions. These my thoughts I found beautifully mirrored in a statement by C. E. Montague, a writer for the *Manchester Guardian* early in this century.

> People gush and moan too much about the loss of ancient buildings of no special note—"landmarks" and "links with the past." In towns, as in

34. Brasilia, the new capital of Brazil.
Architect: Oscar Niemeyer. View from
Presidential Palace to the National Congress
Building. A large new city amidst a virgin
forest laid out for future growth.
Photo: Paolo Muniz, Life.

human bodies, the only state of health is one of rapid wasting and repair. . . . In the great ages of art, buildings have not been regarded as if immortality were their due. It is but an invalidish modern notion that any house which is handsome or has had an illustrious tenant ought to be coddled into the preternatural old age which the Struldbrugs of Gulliver found to be so disappointing. Cities whose health is robust are never content to live, as it were, on their funded capital of achievement in buildings or anything else; they push on; they think more of building well now than of not pulling down. And no cities are so excitingly beautiful as those in which architecture is still alive and at work.

This is the wisdom of a mature man whose love encompasses a whole cycle from past to present, who is accustomed to say "and" instead of "either–or."

Not so our present commentators. The courageous act of creating new cities on virgin ground, for instance, has been deplored as a presumptuous attempt at cheating on the slow course of a natural development. By premature snap judgments, the very idea of attempting a job of such magnitude has been decried. Of course, the initial steps to build a new city can only provide a skeleton which future times will fill in with live tissue and with the cultural humus that will give it its specific character. There are also bound to be formidable digressions from the original concepts since cities rarely rise from pure, unadulterated architectural blueprints; in fact they have usually been shaped—and not always to their detriment—as much by plan as by sheer accidents of an unforeseeable nature with unforeseeable consequences. Loyalty and emotional bonds grow only from active long-term identification with a certain setting and no newly founded city ever started out with it at the beginning. Whatever true shortcomings may be found in a later verdict on cities like Chandigarh or Brazilia, it is the *deed* that counts and should be gratefully acknowledged. Someone must take the initiative, must pour the essence of his life into the new venture, not counting the cost and trust that future generations will carry on. Such confidence was the moral attribute of the great builders of the past from Samara to Constantinople to Kyoto, who all, one day, started from scratch in the middle of nothing. Every vigorous age has had its own vision of urban splendor. Why should we be deprived of it? There is so much in our civilization to be proud of and to permit us to be optimistic that we should end timidity and sentimentality when judging and deciding on its manifestations. The more positive and constructive the attitude of the average citizen will be toward our own period, the better and faster will the custodians of our visual environment, the architects and planners, be able to give it significant order and form. As things stand now, they are duly charged with the task of finding new urbanistic patterns to be superimposed on the chaotic fabric of our cities and towns, but they are neither given support by the people nor the power of decision.

This confusion and paralysis have arisen because the average citizen, ignorant or uninterested in the visual aspects of his civic background, does not participate in the attempts to solve environmental urban problems. He is not aware of his coresponsibility nor of his own power in a democracy to make his voice count. But now that our material Utopia has arrived and we are largely free of want and relieved from heavy physical toil by our machines and by automation, he should be able to bring his intellectual and spiritual potential to full fruition. This needs, of course, a great educational effort. Only through education, still the greatest challenge of life, can the public's receptivity to cultural interests be sharpened and eventually be channeled into new group consciousness. Communication between maker and user would thus be restored and the fear and hysteria which have gripped so many unfortified minds today may give way to constructive participation and response.

In the absence of such a state of mutual response and of commonly valid standards, the best an honest designer can do is to contribute to the development of such standards by taking the most direct, straightforward approach in solving his problems. This may seem like a self-evident demand, but it has become, in fact, almost a rarity nowadays. In explaining such a direct approach I had better begin by stating what it is *not.* The word "direct" here is not meant to stand for the expressionistic immediacy of momentary inspiration. It describes, rather, the attitude of a man who has been able to empty his mind of prejudice and all nonessential considerations and has thereby arrived at a state of new innocence which allows him to penetrate to the very core of his task. Knowing that significant form does not originate at the beginning of a design process, he embarks on a passionate search for an answer in which all relevant factors—social, visual, technical, and economic—have been brought into balance. The

35. The Parthenon on the Acropolis in Athens. The great cultural building rises above the city and all its buildings; it dominates by its position, its scale, and its proportions. The neighboring buildings keep a respectful distance.

original impulse for the design may come from anyone of these provinces, but it takes long and systematic training to get into the habit of seeing all factors involved simultaneously and in their mutual relationships so that one proceeds concentrically instead of sectorially. The famous demand to design "from the inside out" is just as one-sided as that of designing "from the outside in." Rigidly applied, either approach leads to artificial manipulation of space and form, that is, to formalism of one kind or another. Instead, the architect should make a constant attempt to reconcile opposites—the inward and the outward, the solid and the void, unity and diversity. Only comprehensive thinking all the way through the designing stage, while keeping a sharp self-discipline and consistently discarding the unessential, will produce a direct and forceful architectural statement. Whether the design result will later be considered a work of art depends on the architect's innate poetic gift to touch off an emotional response in the beholder beyond

36. Vigevano, Italy. View from the air. The dome
dominates the scene amidst the restrained architecture
of residential buildings. The plaza, the open civic
living room, belongs to the pedestrian.

his appreciation of the practical usefulness of a structure. The order arrived at by an extraordinary artist does not present a closed, logical system, as it is found, for instance, in mathematics. It remains rather an open process, a paradox in suspense, eternally unfathomable, and therefore forever fascinating. We need only remember the systems of seemingly logical sequences of proportion in Greek temples which were in some instances suddenly and unaccountably disregarded by their architects. *The immeasurable, the irrational, the unaccounted for in a work of art seem to be its immortal ferment which makes it unique.* This cannot be described or taught. It *is!* It makes the phenomena of life and life's continuity comprehensible to death-bound man, and it creates the milestones of tradition.

After I have tried here to outline an approach to design as I see it, I want to put the greatest emphasis again on the necessity to integrate every new building, its shape and scale of design, with the environment of which it will be a part and to give it a character commensurate with its proper place in the social order.

Such an attitude of consideration toward the whole environment, combined with an unprejudiced, fresh design approach, represents a true sense of tradition and respect for continuity. To develop this attitude in the new generation of architects would seem to me the foremost goal of architectural education.

I should like to leave you with the words of the modern Greek poet George Seferis, which might serve as a memento to every architect:

> All I want is to speak simply;
>   for this grace I pray
> For we have loaded down even
>   the song with so many kinds
>   of music
> That gradually it sinks.
> And our art we so decorated
>   that beneath the gilt
> Its face is eaten away.
> And it is *now* time for us to
>   say the few words we have
>   to say
> Because tomorrow our soul sets
>   sail.

Architecture in Japan

Extended version of article in
"Perspecta 3," *The Yale
Architectural Journal*, 1955, and
"Architettura in Giapone" in
Archittetura Cantiere, No. 23,
Milan, 1966

37. Festival Hall in Tokyo, Japan. Architect:
Kunio Maekawa. Concrete structure.
Photo: Akio Kawasumi.

Architecture in Japan

It is a great privilege for a man of mature years to travel around the world and to have the opportunity to compare human activities while trying to discriminate between the essential and the incidental. During the last ten years I have crossed many oceans and continents, so I have had ample opportunity to observe the gradual conversion of many countries from a feudal past into the now familiar pattern of a modern, industrialized society. It has not always been a gratifying experience. I made it a point to find out which countries had succeeded in retaining cultural initiative and an integrated, balanced form of living; and the rewards of my search, except for some remote and primitive societies, were few and far between. Everywhere the impact of the machine age had created so much confusion that the disadvantages of the conversion were much more in evidence than the advantages.

One of my trips took me to Japan. The first question I was asked by the customs official was: "Are you engaged in culture?" I am indeed "engaged in culture," but the question had never been put to me so bluntly at an airport. It made me wonder, more than ever, exactly what happens when an old culture like the Japanese meets head on with a civilization that has decided to abandon most of the cultural values of a preindustrial era in favor of a new *Weltanschauung* based on science and technique. Though this has enabled us to raise the material standards of living to unprecedented heights, it has, as yet, often failed to enlist the emotional loyalties of the very peoples who developed it. In view of the many split personalities among us, those whose minds dwell in the past where their emotional life is concerned, but who employ the latest technical devices in their professional lives, I wonder whether we are able to provide some of the answers to questions which a thoughtful Oriental might put to us. I got the impression that the Western mind, in its restless desire to seek new horizons in the physical world, would do well to learn a lesson in spiritual intensification from the Oriental mind, i.e., how to seek new horizons in the inner world. We should compare with each other the deeper motives of our existence, to be able to find out what unites us rather than what divides us. For the physical world has become too small for us to be able to afford ignorance of each other, ignorance which inevitably leads to violence. If we share our native gifts, we may yet be able to build a more durable order for the man of the twentieth century than has seemed possible before.

Uppermost in my mind, as a traveling architect, has been the question, "What can artists, architects, and planners contribute to a new cultural unity?" How can they overcome that piecemeal development of our physical surroundings which so often offends?

I have never seen a better example of an integrated culture than in Japan. The reason for the profundity of the old Japanese culture is probably the fact that there was a period when the country had not been disturbed by wars from outside for over a thousand years, and that, for all that time, it had been under about the same type of government. This culture has become so deep-rooted and ramified that

even today the plain man and the farmer still exemplify it subconsciously. A desire to create beauty, for instance, a cultural factor of great importance more and more lacking in the Western world, is still shared by most of the Japanese people. This and other attitudes have become part of the Japanese character and cannot be easily eradicated; they should be looked at as positive factors, with dynamic potentialities that ought to be combined with those qualities and features of Western culture which will make them stronger. East and West must adapt their attitudes and enrich each other, discarding what is weak and obsolete on both sides. The almost exclusive concern with science and its material realizations in the Western world has brought about such a pauperization of other fields of human endeavor that a better understanding of Oriental culture might also help to reinstate neglected values and open our eyes to experiences that are now missing in our lives.

38. Kurashiki, Province of Okayama, Japan. View of the town. Organic unity of the town pattern combined with individual diversity (identical roof angles and materials, but varying proportions). *Photo: Walter Gropius.*

39. Living room of the Imperial Katsura Villa in Kyoto (1620–1624). All walls are sliding. Floor covered with Tatami mats in modular pattern. Natural wood and cream-colored paper on walls give neutral background to colorful clothing worn in seventeenth century. *Photo: Yasuhiro Ishimoto.*

It had always attracted and interested me that a very strong common denominator of form expression had been attained in Japan without, however, stifling individual variation. I had found, if only in illustrations, that the old handmade Japanese house had already all the essential features required today for a modern prefabricated house, namely, modular coordination—the standard mat (a unit of about 3′ × 6′), and movable wall panels. It deeply moved me, therefore, to come finally face to face with these houses in their natural setting. They represented a culture still alive which, in the past, had already found the answer to many of our modern requirements of simplicity, of outdoor–indoor relation, of modular coordination, and, at the same time, of variety of expression, and had thereby attained a common form language uniting all individual efforts. All this was based, of course, on handicrafts, which we know are losing their foothold in our modern world and also in Japan—and which eventually will be replaced by industrial methods and tools. The advantage for the Japanese in today's transitional development seems to be that they are still attuned to and in the presence of perfect examples of the balance achieved between individual initiative and subordination under a common principle. This should enable them to make the otherwise so painful and difficult transition from a handicraft to a machine culture with greater ease and without the loss of orientation, direction, and tradition which is threatening so many other societies.

During my stay in the East, I found again and again that the typically Western approach to a problem, which usually takes the direction of trying to find the most practical, rational, hygienic solution, covers very little ground in the Orient. Past associations; deference to historically meaningful symbols; consideration of beauty and propriety; the recently developed urge to express one's individuality (something new in the East); the wish to catch up with Western civilization and at the same time resentment of Western domination and influence— all these things mingle and counteract each other and make it difficult for anyone, Easterner or Westerner, to work out a common platform from which to operate.

What particularly struck me in Japan is the fact that the cultural strata of over a thousand years reaches more clearly into present day life than in other countries, and I think no one can understand or predict Japanese reactions at all properly who does not bear this in mind. One of the earliest examples of Japanese architecture is the Ise Shrine. This temple is the oldest sanctum of the Shinto religion; its origin goes back into legendary times and is connected with the history of the Japanese Imperial House. Up to the present day the shrine is completely rebuilt every twenty years so that it is always found in a state of utter perfection. They have never been content to repair unsightly parts, but whenever the wooden exterior, the rush-covered roof, or the gilded portions showed signs of decay the whole building was newly constructed on a neighboring site. The newly perfected shrine which contains the relics can only be seen from afar, as it is closed in by several gates through which only the Emperor is allowed to pass. We were permitted, though, to see the old shrine, which gave me a chance to study the oldest building methods of the country, and I was fascinated by the absolute perfection of every detail.

The treatment of the wood surfaces, even on the exterior, is done with such refinement as we would only apply for the finest interior work, and the gold-capped ends of the wood construction look very precious. I was told that it has become difficult to find the enormous trees necessary for this kind of construction, but the Building In- spector told me hopefully that in two hundred years they would be fully supplied again. Three hundred carpenters had worked ten years to complete the new shrine.

The approach to the Ise Shrine is an impressive experience in itself. Shrines and temples in Japan are always surrounded by mag- nificent trees and here the towering Cryptomeria, Hinoki, and Camphor trees, which can be compared only to the gigantic American sequoias, raise their powerful silhouettes out of the flat countryside near the Pacific coast.

Another old Shinto shrine of the year 1241, Itsukushima, is near Hiroshima. The approach here leads through a so-called Torii, the large, wooden gate that everywhere indicates the entrance to a sanc- tum. In this case it has been placed in the water of the Japanese Inland Sea which, at rising tide, surrounds the buildings.

Most Westerners have been led to believe that Japanese architecture is only a branch of the Chinese, but such a view is just as erroneous as if we decided to see in the various North European cultures only modifications of a Greek–Roman original without independent fea- tures. It is true that the contact with the Chinese mainland and with Korea influenced the early Japanese architecture strongly. For instance, the Buddhistic temples in Nara, the oldest imperial city of Japan, were built after the Chinese influence had become strong, and one can easily recognize the change in the approach to the whole layout of the buildings. A straight axis leads toward the center of the build- ing, and everything is arranged in strict symmetry to create the desired atmosphere of divine perfection. The biggest Buddha in the world is enshrined here in the so-called Daibutsu, one of the temples of the Todaiji monastery which was built for the first time in 752 and sub- sequently completely reconstructed after two destructions by fire. This last version is from the year 1709. The heavy wood construction has withstood many earthquakes and typhoons because it supports the big loads never in just one point, but distributes them into a whole system of supports. The enormous structure is quite overpowering and impressive, even though only just large enough to house the Buddha statue which weighs 452 tons. Originally the temple had been built as a symbol for peace, and, during its seven-year construction pe-

40. The Ise Shrine, south of Nagoya, is the oldest
relic of Shintoism. Its origin goes back to the fifth
century. It is rebuilt exactly as the original every
twenty years to keep it in perfect condition. Sublime
craftsmanship. Roofs of cedar bark. All end pieces of
the wood construction (Hinoki) have gilded metal
shoes. Venerable old cedar trees (Cryptomeria) surround
the fenced-in temple place.
Photo: Richard Haag.

41. "Torii" of the Shinto temple
Itsukushima near Hiroshima
(thirteenth century). Built of
camphor wood, painted bright red,
it symbolizes the gate to heaven.
Photo: Walter Gropius.

42. Entrance to the Imperial Katsura Villa in Kyoto, Japan. The pavement strip, leading to the Villa, gives intimate scale by avoiding axial direction and symmetry. *Photo: Yasuhiro Ishimoto.*

riod, the imperial court as well as the townspeople were brought near financial ruin. But a seventy-year peace period actually followed this effort.

After this first strong impact of Chinese Buddhist influence, the Japanese began to develop their own independent aesthetic philosophy which often expressed itself in contrast to the Chinese conception. The Japanese residential house and the tea house show these strong independent characteristics particularly well: no symmetry, which is strictly reserved for the temple as a symbol of divine perfection; no straight, imposing axes, but, instead, surprise effects and stimulation by subtly changing directions in the approaches to buildings; emphasis on human scale throughout, combined with openness and flexibility of plan. These are timeless virtues which could be utilized today with our new technical means, even better than during the centuries of the crafts.

We can understand the architecture of nations and periods only as we win an inside knowledge of their way of thinking and their philosophy. The Japanese architects have been deeply influenced by the

43. Dwelling of a priest in the Samboin temple in Kyoto, Japan. Its famous garden was allegedly designed by the Dictator Hideyoshi.
Photo: Walter Gropius.

44. Jakoin Nunnery near Kyoto, Japan. Since the twelfth century it has been standing in the peaceful seclusion of the mountains. Behind the white square, the window shutters, used only during the night, are hidden.
Photo: Walter Gropius.

Zen sect, which started in China as a Buddhist sect and was influenced by Confucianism and Taoism, creeds which overlap in Asiatic countries without creating much antagonism to each other. The Zen creed never became very popular in China, while the Japanese embraced it wholeheartedly and allowed their conduct of life to be strongly formed by it. Zen teaches a human ideal of self-education by Spartan means. At its start it was a very aristocratic creed. It would therefore probably have remained largely unpopular with the masses but for its genius of expressing conviction in a very direct way, going straight to the heart of the matter and manifesting itself in action rather than confining itself to speculative thinking and meditation only. It was a way of self-perfection which gave enormous effectiveness to whatever philosophical conviction an individual might have happened to acquire. It became popular first with the war lords and samurais who, in their hazardous life during the period of rival fighting when the Emperor had lost his power to the shoguns, looked for a discipline that would enable them to become impervious to danger and invulnerable to the vagaries of fate. This influence could still be detected, in its radical form, in the suicidal Kamikaze pilots of World War II. But it also inspired the tea ceremony, which has formed the Japanese character of all classes by its example of simplicity combined with acute awareness of values. It is much more than a tea ceremony, it is expressive of a whole way of life, and every visitor to Japan can still feel its influence. There is something extraordinary in the fact that Japanese culture, which has had centuries of time to ripen and to go through various stages without being interrupted by foreign domination and influence, has culminated in a cult of utter simplicity and austerity. Nothing in this simplicity is left to chance, however. We with our casual, offhand manner must often appear to the Japanese as so many unformed youngsters who go to an incredible waste of material because they have never learned the significance of economy in matter and spirit, coming, as they do, from a civilization which produces the present overabundance of haphazard shapes and forms.

I was amazed to discover how strong the influence of the tea ceremony has been on all traditional architectural concepts: undemonstrative noble austerity, most discriminating use of simple, well-formed tools, restrained use of color in the tea houses, and carefully planned gardens. The tea ceremony itself, though still regularly performed by the older generation, has changed into a simple tea party for the younger set, but the spirit remains even now. It has given dignity to poverty, and its example is probably accountable for the extraordinary morale people display even when they find themselves in the most adverse conditions.

Nowadays the young Japanese themselves are fed up with this self-imposed economy of means and have begun to revolt against this setting of "noble poverty." What delights our eye has become to them a symbol of failure to provide more comfort and convenience, and they argue that their simplicity is not voluntary but imposed by circumstances. Whatever truth there is in this, it will be an unspeakable loss to all who have strong artistic inclinations if the introspective

45. "Hokkedo," oldest building of the Todai-ji-temple in Nara, Japan, still intact (733).
Photo: Asuka-en, Nara.

form of Japanese life should give way entirely to our indulgence in material pursuits and to our rather shallow addiction to change for change's sake. It would be a very different matter if the achievements of Japanese tradition were representative only of a feudal past; as it is, they are still pregnant with unrealized potentialities.

Right now the young generation in Japan is ready to cast away everything that determined the past. I have listened with sorrow to their self-abuse. Of course, we have to bear in mind that Zen Buddhism provides no answer to the social problem of human relations which is uppermost in everyone's mind today. Its conviction that it is impossible to raise the standard of living without impairing its quality, and that one can improve his lot only by robbing his brother, preparing, thereby, the way for retaliation and war, is no longer tenable. Science, branded by Zen Buddhism for its analytical, purely intellectual character, has made it possible to raise the material standard of living without lowering its spiritual quality. That this latter possibility is not generally realized and applied does not detract from its validity and only proves that we are morally weak and addicted to old prejudices. Certainly Zen, in its old form, with its old social associations, has become unsatisfactory for the present generation, but, stripped of its incrustations and rejuvenated, it could reveal its sound and vital substance.

One point of the Zen philosophy interests me particularly, namely, *that it considers artistic impulses more basic, more innate than ethical ones and therefore of more permanent, primary importance. It takes morality to be only regulative, but art to be creative.* So Zen finds its inevitable association with art, though a strict moral code, is taken for granted. In contrast to the Western Puritan, the Zen disciple learns to control his emotions, not to suppress them.

At the end of innumerable discussions with a score of architects in a Japanese inn near the Fujiyama, I closed our discussion by quoting sound Zen advice which had impressed me very much: "Develop an infallible technique, and then place yourself at the mercy of inspiration." This underlines the Zen abhorrence of purely intellectual reasoning ("the logical impasse," as they call it) and the emphasis on spontaneous response to direct experience. My own trend of thought, as exemplified in the Bauhaus, was here startlingly confirmed.

Some people have ventured to say that the modern European–American movement in architecture has been strongly influenced by the Japanese conception. The truth is that the extraordinary visual manifestations of the old Japanese culture, and the twentieth-century architectural conception of the West, originated independently from very different premises. The Japanese approach was based on an age-old, articulate philosophy which had thoroughly permeated and formed the living habits of its society. Our Western approach is a new beginning, taking the first initial steps toward a new integration of thought and action in a changing world, a singularly chaotic world, confused by too many great, but still-undigested discoveries in the scientific and psychological fields and only tenuously connected by philosophical or religious principles.

Also the Japanese had been favored with a climate less harsh and intimidating than that of the northern parts of the West and with the

46. Room in the teahouse (Shokintei) of the Imperial Katsura Villa in Kyoto, Japan. Outdoor–indoor relation achieved by sliding exterior walls of wood frame and translucent paper. *Photo: Walter Gropius.*

splendid isolation of an insular position which kept out invaders. Therefore, they came to employ certain desirable design features, like the openness of the house, long before they could be introduced in the West. It was only recently that industrial advances began to make available new technical means which permitted Western architects to overcome the defensive character that Western houses had assumed through centuries of relentless warfare or relentless winters.

These factors may explain the surprising kinship between the old Japanese and the new Western architectural approach, factors which differ greatly from a superficial and imitative transfer of style characteristics from the one to the other. The traditional house is so strikingly modern because it contains perfect solutions, already centuries old, for problems which the contemporary Western architect is still wrestling with today, i.e., complete flexibility of movable exterior and interior walls, changeability and multiuse of spaces, modular coordination of all the building parts, and prefabrication. Today, one can still buy in Japan all the handmade standardized component parts of

47. Farmhouse near Osaka, Japan. Interior with the typical, flexible sliding window wall. Sixteenth century. *Photo: Yoshimura.*

a wooden house on the market and assemble them on the site. The flexibility of use of these component parts is so great that they can satisfy the seemingly self-contradictory requirement of providing unity and diversity of form expression at the same time. Such an achievement of continuity is always indicative of great depth and ramification of the cultural development.

But nowadays the young Japanese architect is often ready to sacrifice all these advantages because to him they are associated with the feudal past and its lack of privacy and individual independence. His new love is the unpenetrable, unmovable concrete wall which seems to embody for him the strength and sturdiness he wants to give to his modern dwellings. He is apt to forget in his enthusiasm that the humid warmth of a Japanese summer demands the airiest of enclosures, and that only expensive insulation methods would offset the inherent disadvantages of the solid concrete wall for housing purposes.

The indoor–outdoor relation between house and garden, which has only been so recently "discovered" in the West, was a matter of great concern in Japan centuries ago. Openings, terraces, and balconies were placed with an eye to the landscape and far and near scenery. Most of the gardens were designed to be looked at from the terraces that surround the house or temple, not to be used for picnics or rough games. These terraces of smooth, glistening wood are protected by a roof overhang and lifted off the ground by wooden supports as protection against the dampness of the rainy season. People sit and children play on these terraces and look down into the gardens which open up a world of imagination and invention for the contemplative onlooker. They are accessible from the rooms by big sliding doors. One of the most attractive and modern features of the traditional house are the vistas across various rooms at different angles and, then, out into the garden.

Japanese man-made landscape and gardens are as beautiful as they are because a deep understanding of nature has been all-prevailing in the country. I believe that the Japanese approach of persuading and stimulating nature will have a greater future value than the predominant Western method of conquering and exploiting her.

I was driving once through a small place in the vicinity of Tokyo, when, at one point, our car was momentarily blocked by a large,

48. Ryoanji Rockgarden, designed by the Zen priest
Soami at the end of the fifteenth century. Fifteen
carefully selected rocks stand in raked white gravel
against a quiet wall.
Photo: Walter Gropius.

beautiful tree standing awkwardly in the highway. It bore a big sign which, my interpreter explained to me, said: "Let's love this tree." It had been put up by the townspeople who felt they just couldn't part with this impressive creation for the sake of traffic.

Beautiful gardens are by no means found only around temples or big country estates. In fact the particular ingenuity of the Japanese gardener is that he can turn even a tiny court between two rooms into an imaginative, enchanting area. Wedged in between city houses, in back of diminutive restaurants, in odd lots that would be nothing but dumping places in our towns, one comes upon the most exquisite plant arrangements and beautifully trimmed trees. Where green nature cannot be easily accommodated, rocks are placed in such arresting patterns that they transform an insignificant space into a magical one. The Japanese are very partial to stones and rocks. What, in the beginning, may have been a very practical arrangement to keep paths dry during the inundations of the rainy season has become a real art which is so ubiquitously applied that it has now become necessary to prohibit by the law the indiscriminate removal of rocks from river-beds and the open landscape.

One of my really overwhelming experiences was a visit to the Ryoanji rockgarden, a garden belonging to a Zen monastery in Kyoto (1480). Photographs cannot convey the magic of this place. It is a large rectangle backed by a long, low wall with sloping dark grey tile coping and flanked by similar walls and a building opposite the long wall. One looks down on the rockgarden from the wooden terrace along the reception hall of the monastery; it is only 30′ × 79′. The first reaction upon entering this charmed area is speechlessness. What you see is fifteen well chosen rocks put in the white gravel that covers the entire place. The gravel is painstakingly raked into parallel lines except for the areas directly around the stones, where the gravel is raked into a wavy pattern. The absence of any time-bound, man-made object, or of plants, takes the garden out of the realm of perishable values; and the simplicity of the stones, which are by no means of exceptional beauty, but have been chosen with a keen eye for proportion, keeps the composition from oversophistication. The scale is truly monumental in spite of its insignificant size. A feeling of complete peace, though not of stifled imagination, is created because the stones, in their relative sizes, look more like indications of potential forces, of a balanced tension, which occupy and stimulate the mind.

The Japanese writer Hasegawa has observed that the cultural growth of traditional Japanese art has been democratic in character even though it took place under feudal regimes. This is true indeed. The house and the garden of the common man and that of a monastery, a prince, or even the Emperor, reveal the same spirit of approach. They differ in size and quality and treatment of materials but not in their basic conception, as the equivalent buildings did during the feudal times in Europe.

In contrast to our Western idea of the Japanese "paper house," the peasant houses are not only of extraordinary beauty but also of considerable solidity. The family—or, rather, clan—spirit is very strong, and the building of a house is a responsibility shouldered by all members of such a clan. In this way it has been possible to keep up a standard of excellence in the country which has been entirely lost in the modern big cities. In the clean, small villages one never sees dirty, neglected farmsteads, unrepaired roofs or untidy dumping places; everywhere trees and bushes grow luxuriantly, and the peasants themselves, in their traditional garb, give the whole picture its colorful accents.

If we compare these humble buildings to the elegant dwellings of the former ruling classes, we find basically the same features, only polished and refined to suit a higher, more sophisticated standard of living.

The most illustrious example of this democratic spirit is the Katsura Imperial Villa in Kyoto. It was begun in 1620, by a team working under the spiritual influence of the great tea master Kobori Enshu. Though its owner was an imperial prince, there is no pomp, no superfluous luxury; with great simplicity and restraint of means, a truly noble edifice has been created in which a sense of freedom and peace resides as an inherent quality. We feel tremendously attracted to this building even now because man and his way of living were the focus of its conception. No vanity, no pretentious monumentalism were in the mind of the designers, but only the desire to create a balanced container for beautiful living.

The teamwork of the Katsura Villa, for which the records still exist,

49. Farmhouse east of
Tokyo, Japan. Natural
wood frame, stucco panels
whitewashed, paper
screens, thatched roof
of cedar bark.
Photo: Walter Gropius.

50. Farmhouse east of
Tokyo, Japan. Natural
wood frame, stucco panels
whitewashed, paper
screens. In spite of its
lightness the construction
is remarkably sturdy.
Photo: Walter Gropius.

shows a sound integration of designer and builder when compared to the fatal separation of design and execution from which our present architectural profession suffers. The building and its immediate surroundings are one homogeneous, integrated space composition; no static conception, no symmetry, no central focus in the plan. Space, here the only medium of artistic creation, appears to be magically floating.

Most characteristic of the spirit of the conception is the path to the entrance gate of the villa. It conforms to the favorite Zen approach, which is rarely direct, axial, and symmetrical. There is a decided distaste for the imposing straight avenue; instead, there is a preference for the intimate and casual but carefully planned approach which supplies surprises at every turn and leads up to the main objective in a human, natural, unimposing manner.

The spirit of the design conception, particularly that of the early part of the building, the Old Shoin, is one of remarkable clarity. The skill in the workmanship is just as remarkable as that in the methods of design. The structure is a simple skeleton of post and beams; almost all exterior and interior walls are movable and nonstructural. The wind-bracing is placed invisibly under the roof, while strong hidden joints make the structure typhoon-proof.

The modular coordination used at this period was the most subtle known, more so than that of the Egyptians, even more than that of the Greeks. The rooms were laid out on a multiple of a standard mat, the Tatami (about 3′ x 6′); all the building parts were dimensioned horizontally and vertically on a multiple of the column thickness, which varied with the size of spaces and their respective spans.

The living spaces are modest in size, in keeping with the human scale. The use of movable partitions and window frames makes their proportions extremely variable. The accentuated emptiness of the rooms with their subdued walls is a deliberately intended factor of design; its purpose is to put the emphasis on the human figure and support it with a sympathetic background. As in most Japanese creations, we find here also a predilection for clear contrasts: against the austere purity of the architectural frame, the spontaneous, sketchlike painting and the wealth of magnificent garments; against the light, transparent house construction, the heavy, sculptural roof. The use of contrasting materials which enhance each other in their effectiveness had been devel-

51. Main view of the Katsura Imperial Villa in Kyoto; built 1620–1624 for Prince Toshihito by a team of designers and craftsmen who worked under the spiritual influence of the famous teamaster Kobori Enshu. Form and material of refined simplicity. The most mature and consummate example of Japanese architecture and garden design.
Photo: Walter Gropius.

oped early, and nowhere does one find an attempt at "matching" by identical forms and colors (one of our American preoccupations), but always great care in complementing, relating, and counterbalancing. Man's oneness with nature is expressed by the use of materials left in their natural colors and by a worship of the occasional deliberately unfinished detail, corresponding to the irregularities in nature. For only the incomplete was considered to be still part of the fluid process of life; symmetry, the symbol of perfection, was reserved for the temple. The aesthetic effect is a pure, architectonic one, achieved by simple contrasts of bright and dark, smooth and rough and by juxtaposition of plain squares, rectangles, and stripes. However, none of these means are aesthetic abstractions; they are all meaningful realities, related to daily life. The builder subordinated himself and his work to the supra-individual idea of a unified environment and thereby avoided the traps of vanity, the *nouveauté,* and the stunt. This is the lofty abode of man in equilibrium, in serenity.

52. "Karamon," the gate of the Toshoga Shrine, Nikko, Japan. Memorial for the powerful Tokugawa Family, 1634-1636. Overloaded, baroque form, at the same time of highly perfected craftsmanship.

Characteristically, this attitude of restraint had, during the same period, its counterpart in the ostentatious display of the mausoleum of the powerful Tokugawa shoguns at Nikko. Tremendous skill in craftsmanship was misused here by the shoguns to glorify themselves in an overbearing profusion of ornament and decoration, which destroys the clarity of the architectural composition as a whole and leaves an impress of conceit and self-praise.

In contrast, the sublime architectural expression of the Katsura Villa has an impact on the spectator which lifts him unfailingly onto a high spiritual plane. Representing the human ideals and virtues of the Japanese society and its recognized style of living, the Katsura Villa exemplifies the very peak of architectural development. Perhaps it is the aristocratic tradition on the one hand, and the more earthbound, elemental features of the plain farmhouse on the other, which, combined in this unique design, have earned it its fame. Its influence remained predominant for rural and urban houses alike until Western civilization began to confuse this powerful tradition.

It must be admitted, though, that even the Katsura Villa shows some traces of decline which we should recognize lest we fail to discriminate with the fullest clarity between the essential and the incidental features of this edifice, and thereby fail to judge properly its influence on Japanese tradition as well as on our modern architecture wherever it searches for new visual expression. The Villa was built in three sections over a span of thirty-eight years, and, though its irregularly staggered ground plan and its structural elements keep the same strong and pure spirit throughout, in its last-built section, the New Goten (1968), the purity of conception is obscured a little by some added-on ornamental elements in the interior, like the all-too-sophisticated bronze hardware on and above the sliding doors, the purely decorative "ramma" panels, the too-elaborate shelves and cabinets, and the Chinese window in the First Room.

If we judge by the highest standards, we may also find some weak points in the Katsura's garden. Though its intimate spaces, its pavements, and its plantings are of enchanting beauty, the overemphasis on playful details sometimes impairs the continuity and coherence of the spatial conception as a whole. The importance given to overcrowded rock compositions, mainly around the Shokintei Teahouse, reminds me of the age-old Japanese art of *bon-seki*, consisting of a tray, filled with sand, in which pebbles of different size and color are arranged in artful compositions.

However, nothing can detract from the great lesson this true architectural masterwork still offers us today. The Katsura Villa appeals to our emotions because here, for once, design has been linked closely to the human being, to his style of life, and to the realities of his existence. Only wise, experienced minds could have conceived so great an example of the Japanese genius for creating architectural space of truly human scale.

As part of a long development of an established style of living, the architectural mold of the Japanese dwelling became basically fixed. In the end it attained such balanced perfection that the creative imagination of architects spent itself in ever more subtle artistry of details,

53. House of architect
Kenzo Tange in Tokyo,
1953.
Photo: Ch. Hirayama.

and no attempt was made to change the basic approach. The infinite artistic potentialities, provided by the inexhaustible flexibility of the system and its spirit, gave it an unequaled permanence which nobody dared to challenge. On the contrary, to abide by its powerful tradition and to channel one's own creative impulses into the same direction became the unquestioned virtue of designers and builders.

So deeply was I impressed by the Japanese architecture of the past that, to the surprise of my Japanese colleagues who, knowing me as a rebel and an innovator, expected me to act accordingly, I continually urged them not to cast wholly overboard the great spirit of their traditional architecture, for I feel it to be still full of unrealized potentialities for our modern way of life.

Yet the problem the modern Japanese faces is formidable. If he looks into the older parts of a town, he still finds there a medieval setup—streets which belong to various guilds, small shops where the goods

54. Aquarium by architect Motoo Take,
built of concrete and brick.

which are produced by the family in the back room are sold off, narrow lanes that are impossible to enter by automobile.

In contrast to this old world are the new parts of town where people more often than not wear modern Western clothes and where the streets show the same disrupted, untidy, formless pattern as our own. Torn between their devotion to tradition on the one side and the temptation to throw themselves unreservedly into the new adventure on the other, bewildered by foreign ideologies and by a new constitution which suddenly transformed a military dictatorship into a modern democracy, they stand in a whirlpool of problems.

The main difficulty, of course, is overpopulation. The gradual cheapening of everything under this pressure is disheartening to watch, particularly in a country where one is surrounded everywhere by the high standards of the past. In the not yet fully industrialized economic setup of Japan, children are important, because almost all shop owners and all peasants run their places with the help of their children, not of employees. Also, in the absence of public welfare institutions, old people depend entirely on their children for their support. But while there was formerly a very high death rate for infants, now, under the influence of hygiene and medical progress, the death rate has been so much lowered that a frightening increase in population has taken place (although the birthrate is still lower than that of the United States) which is accelerated by the tremendous number of repatriates from Korea and other former Japanese possessions.

Before World War II, Japan owned about 260,000 square miles, of which she has lost 46 percent. Of this land, only 15.5 percent is arable and consequently not enough food can be produced; even a certain amount of rice must be imported. About 80 percent of the raw materials for industry has to be bought abroad. When Admiral Perry entered the country in 1855, there were 27 million people; now there are 88 million.

The Japanese architect, in particular, faces the almost insoluble task of having to house a population whose way of life, particularly in the cities, is in the process of a far-reaching transformation. Apart from the fact that he is forced to work within very limited means, he is also frustrated by the fact that a compromise between the traditional Japanese and the modern Western living habits, which is unavoidable

55. Town hall in Hashima by architect Junzo Sakakura.
View from south with entrance ramp.
Photo: Y. Futagawa.

nowadays, presents him with the most difficult psychological and technical problems. In the traditional house people lived in comparatively small rooms which were free of the profusion of interior paraphernalia cluttering up our living spaces. No chairs, no beds, only some low tables and cushions on the mats; for sleeping, thick, mattress-like pads are placed on the floor, to be taken away again in the daytime so that none of the space is wasted. If Western style living, which is gradually becoming more and more accepted in Japan now, is introduced into this finely balanced interior, space-consuming chairs and beds will simply explode the modest, dignified frame and ruin the proportions. So the architect faces the dilemma either to have to jam modern bulky furniture into a small traditional house, the parts of which he can still procure on the normal market for a low price, or to have to increase the size of the house considerably by adopting a Western plan at a time when economical difficulties make it almost prohibitive for clients to accept such a solution.

The introduction of heating, unknown in the old house, causes even greater complications. The traditional wood and paper panels and lacquered goods all crack and warp under the influence of heating. From what I know of the educational principles which prevailed, I believe that the absence of heating devices was not an outcome of uninventiveness but rather of a Spartan inclination in the Japanese people. They have been brought up for so long with the idea that it is more important to develop the spirit than to pamper the body that even today, when this spirit is waning, they are still slow to seize on modern amenities of life, quite apart from the fact that they are often financially unable to afford them.

The majority of all the building parts are still made by hand, using the old materials, mainly wood. This still is the most economical way to build. At a time when everything was in the middle of a postwar depression, and new housing for the lower income groups was likely to be shoddy and makeshift for lack of funds, the modern architect who wanted to introduce a new type of building for new living habits was indeed severely handicapped. The vast army of craftsmen who still produce the entire housing for Japan must find methods of increasing their production by gradually increasing the use of machines; but the economic safety margin is so precarious that attempts at

56. Administration building of the prefecture of
Kagawa, Japan. Architect: Kenzo Tange. Concrete
structure.

57. Town hall in
Kurashiki, Japan.
Architect: Kenzo Tange.
Photo: Y. Futagawa.

58. Town hall in Kurashiki,
Japan. Architect: Kenzo
Tange. Vestibule and main
staircase.
Photo: T. Taira.

59. Memorial for the Dead of Hiroshima, Japan, in the Peace Park of Hiroshima. Architect: Kenzo Tange. In the background, the Museum.

revolutionizing the building industry too quickly would throw too many people out of work and disrupt many habits of living which are still in full command. This, of course, is frustrating in many ways to the modern architects who are waiting impatiently to make use in a broader way of more modern methods and tools.

I believe, though, that in spite of all the present obstacles, the Japanese architect will focus his thinking boldly and without sentimentality on a modern approach to our twentieth-century problems. To arrive at a new, independent conception for their work and to bring about a fertile synthesis of their many, contradictory tendencies, they will need, however, the living elements from the past as well as from the present. Japan is blessed with a precious heritage, an integrated culture whose unity is maintained by the subconscious habits of the people. It still shows that mark of deep and genuine culture, a standard of form so broad that it admits infinite individual variety. I believe that the difficult transformation from a traditional to a modern form of society, adapted to the industrial age, should be carried through by the Japanese in the spirit of their *own* culture; it should be enriched by the new technical achievements of the West, but without submitting entirely to the Western attitude.

There is increasing evidence that such thinking is gaining recognition in Japan and that their best architects have weathered the first, unnerving impact of Western invasion and are now making mature contributions to the development of architecture which are among the very best produced in the world today.

Designing
Museum Buildings

Museum of Fine Arts, Springfield,
Mass., Oct. 16, 1946, for
New England Conference of the
American Association of Museums

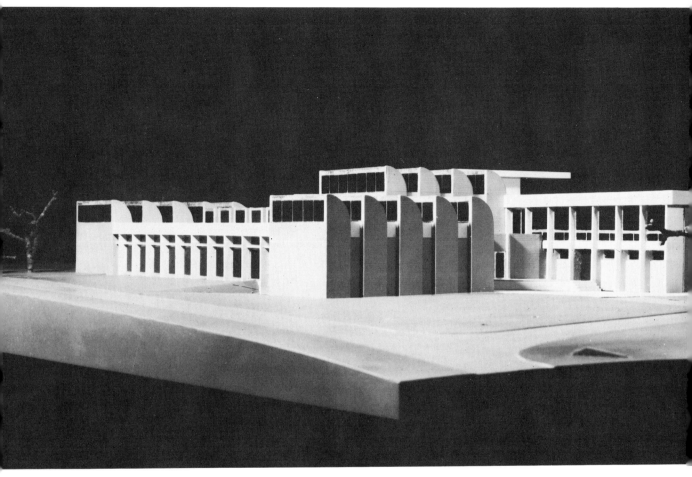

60. Project for the Bauhaus-Archiv, Darmstadt, Germany.
Walter Gropius (The Architects Collaborative).

Designing Museum Buildings

Building is the fulfillment of practical requirements. Architecture interprets the emotional life of man.

A museum building certainly has to be more than a mere receptacle for collections. We expect it to satisfy higher demands, to have what we call a "monumental" expression and, as such, to embody the civic and cultural pride of the community.

This twofold aspect, that of the practical and technical requirements on the one hand, and of the emotional demands on the other—a synthesis of the art of building and the art of architecture—gives the direction in which a critical approach to designing a museum might be organized.*

* This is suggested as a sequence of procedure: Before an architect can start designing a museum, a competent committee should come to terms with its program after a comprehensive research study has been made. The program must contain

I will concentrate particularly on the more intricate problems of scale, flexibility, light, and architectural form expression, all to be seen in relation to the museum's visitor as the principal person to be served. For besides all those practical requirements of space and circulation, the committee should lay down an overall policy of how best to attract people to the museum. This will necessitate a study of the average visitor's psychological makeup, and I believe this to be even more important than the utilitarian aspects involved. All decisions made by the program committee should be checked as to their potential effect on the visitor, for it is he whom we intend to inform, to educate, to entertain. The question is to be raised: How can we create conditions which will make him more receptive and more active?

It is a scientific fact that a human being needs frequently changing impressions in order to keep his receptivity in a state of alertness. Continuity of unaltered conditions, as comfortable as it may be, has a dulling and lulling effect. For instance, traveling for a whole day in an air-conditioned Pullman car of even temperature, air velocity, and humidity makes us uneasy. Even on a very hot day, we like to step out of the train at the station, seeking the contrast of less comfortable conditions, if only for a change. For this will enable us to enjoy again the comfortable air conditioning back in the car. In the same way, the capacity of a visitor to receive the messages of many masterpieces crowded together will dwindle rapidly unless we are able to refresh him frequently. His mind must be neutralized after each impression before a new impression can sink in. We cannot keep him at a high pitch of ecstasy for hours while he is wandering through a gallery; but the acuity of his interest can be kept awake by skillful design offering him ever-varying space and light effects and an arrangement of display, rich in contrasts. Only if he is thus compelled to use

conclusive information as to the site chosen, its accessibility, the potential traffic and parking capacity, the space requirements of the building proper, and the flow diagrams for circulation resulting from a logical analysis of the desired museum activities. The program committee may be composed of the director of the museum, its superintendent, a layman as the client's representative, and an architect, together with a lighting engineer to be commissioned with the design. It appears to be indispensable that the research study should be started in close collaboration with the designer of the building; for this will establish a consistent direction of thought for all participants of the committee. It will improve their mutual understanding and alleviate prejudices of either a practical or an aesthetic kind.

his natural functions of adaptation, will he remain an untired and active participant.

Besides those desirable attractions as lectures and films, the arrangement of reading rooms and study rooms, the exhibition spaces themselves, and the distribution of the exhibits in them should create a sequence of arresting surprises which must be well timed and properly scaled to fit the visitor's susceptibility.

With this demand, we enter the realm of architectural creation. A most common offense in designing public buildings is that committed against the human scale. The size of our human body, of which we are constantly conscious, serves us as a yardstick when perceiving space. The emotional interest of a spectator will fade or be intensified when we decrease or increase the optical scale of an object. I remember the intense physical horror which I experienced when seeing on a screen the enlarged picture of a scorpion and a mantis appearing as huge monsters, tearing each other to pieces in a gruesome life-and-death struggle. Merely through an enlargement of the optical scale, causing a closer emotional relation, strong physical and psychological sensations sprang up which would not have occurred had I seen the fight in its original smaller scale.

The Caesars, playing God, intending to subjugate their subjects by fear, expressed their power by megalomania axes of superhuman scale. Hitler and Mussolini both received in rooms of colossal size, seated at the opposite end of the entrance so that the approaching visitor was made to feel uneasy and humble.

In our democratic civilization where the emphasis is on the freedom of the individual, the architect must not indulge in dictatorial superscale. He has to find monumental expression by means other than intimidation. Today's democratic citizen will act with bored indifference to oversized spaces intended to impress him by mere bigness. Yet a space composition, well related to his natural understanding of space and scale, will invite and attract him.

The essence of all these observations leads me to demand that man should be large in proportion to the architectural spaces. Thus, his biological qualities should determine the scale of the component parts of a museum, not the whims or fantasies of an ever-so-generous Maecenas and his all-too-obedient architect. In short, in a democracy, a public building, as a museum, is meant to serve the visitor, not to dictate to him. Its design should, therefore, avoid all physical and psychological barriers. The building should be a means to an end, not an end in itself; then its scale will be human.

To this demand for the proper human scale, we have to add that of flexibility in a museum building. We have seen that changes and surprise are the essence of enhancing the visitor's alertness. What then can the designer of a museum contribute to make the building flexible and to help keep the museum a living organism?

The rapid changes which have occurred during the last decades have convinced us that the requirements for a museum are changing continuously. But can a dignified, permanent building also be flexible? Yes, by means of well-designed systems of movable partitions and screens, thoroughly worked out technically and easily adjustable. The various departments of the museum should be laid out as large, neutral spaces, enclosed by a permanent shell; whereas the interior space composition could be changed according to needs. Today it is technically feasible to solve the problem of sound absorption and the handling of the movable partitions. In any case, rigidity of arrangements should be avoided for all departments. Doors from room section to room section should be avoided. This will create a desirable continuity of space which will keep the visitor inquisitive and expectant, and this is, after all, our foremost task.

The big problem of how to obtain proper lighting will give the museum program committee even greater headaches. Should windows be used or the various forms of skylights or should one do away altogether with natural light and aim at the windowless museum, only artificially illuminated? Or should they insist on a combination of all these potential methods of illumination? A *Report of the Committee on Art Gallery Lighting of the Illuminating Engineering Society* is an important piece of scientific advice trying to bring order into the many lighting problems with which a museum-builder is faced. It will be a helpful guide for designers of museums as well as for their directors who are responsible for the display. On one basic point, however, I would like to challenge the conclusions of this *Report.* I quote the Committee: "Today any interior gallery can be artificially lighted to better effect than is possible by daylight; and in addition it can always reveal each item in its best

aspect, which is only a fleeting occurrence under natural lighting. . . ."
A fleeting occurrence! Here, I believe, is an erroneous simplification,
for the best available artificial light which tries to bring out all the
advantages of an exhibit is, nevertheless, static. It does not change;
natural light, however, is dynamic, is alive as it changes continuously.
The "fleeting occurrence" caused by the change of light is just what
we desire.

I remember a vivid experience I once had in the Pergamon Museum
in Berlin. To me the light on the temple walls coming from skylights
seemed to be confusing and tiring. But one night, I happened to pass
by when a photographer with a large spotlight moved around to find
a position for a camera shot. I was electrified by the strong effect of
the moving light. All of a sudden the reliefs came to life, and I discovered a new beauty of the sculptures which I had never observed
before.

Then think of the wondrous surprise in a cathedral when a sunbeam,
coming from a window and slowly wandering through the twilight of
the nave, suddenly hits the altar. What a delight for the beholder
in spite of his experiencing only a "fleeting occurrence." Is this not
just the kind of lasting impression we should like to offer also to our
museum visitor?

Two factors, then, seem to be of importance for effective lighting.
The first is the changeability of the light on an exhibit regarding its
direction, its intensity, and its color; for this changeability would appeal
to our natural functions of adaptation and would relieve the deadening
effect of any ever-so-perfect static light. Second, if the general artificial
lighting of an exhibition space is kept dim, and strong light is concentrated on exhibits only, avoiding direct glare, the visitor's mind—
free from distraction—will be receptive and concentrated.

Science and industry are not yet advanced enough to fulfill all
lighting requirements. One day we may have at our disposal moving,
man-made sunlight to be used at will, varying in quantity and quality.
However, as long as artificial light cannot yet fully comply with our
requirements, we will have to seek a combination of artificial and
natural light.

According to the *Report on Art Gallery Lighting* mentioned above,
three main factors of light have to be considered for proper illumination

of three-dimensional exhibits such as sculpture and models. This holds for daylight as well as for artificial illumination: first, the main light from the sun and the sky, second, the secondary light in the form of reflection from higher portions of the setting, as a nearby wall, and third, diffused reflection from the lower part of the surroundings, as from floors. The reflecting surfaces of walls and floors have to be of equal concern to us as the main source of light.

I have come to the conclusion that, for any exhibit, particularly for other than two-dimensional pictures, windows as a light source still can offer a legitimate solution. Not only will a glance through a window on the outside help to neutralize the visitor's mind and prepare him for new impressions, but a daylight window also offers the inestimable factor of change in illumination according to the change of weather.

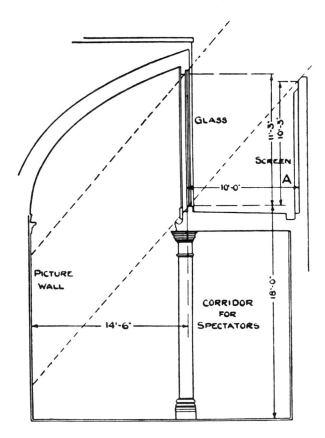

61. Tate Gallery, London. System of Illumination. Indirect daylight, favorable for paintings or three-dimensional exhibits. The eyes of the spectator are shaded under the mezzanine ceiling. From above it, the full daylight illuminates the exhibits, which however remain protected against direct sunlight by a free-standing wall.

As long as we make the best of both natural and artificial light, we shall obtain the relatively greatest surprise effect for the visitor.

My last point of reference concerns the architectural expression of museum buildings. How can a synthesis of the art of building and the art of architecture be achieved? It has been said that, as poetry is the noble development of language, architecture is the noble development of building. As literature has to use the elements of spoken language, architecture has to rely on the structural elements of its period. We cannot speak a language without having agreed first on an alphabet and grammar.

The elements of construction at the disposal of the contemporary architect differ greatly from those of former generations. Steel and concrete skeletons, bridging of wide spans, cantilevered hovering

62. Bauhaus-Archiv, Darmstadt, Germany. System of Illumination. By Walter Gropius, 1964. (The Architects Collaborative). Optional arrangement: either skylight from shed roof for free-standing architectural models and other three-dimensional exhibits, or artificial light, with ceilings closed, for light-sensitive objects. Natural light or its combination with electric spotlights is preferred.

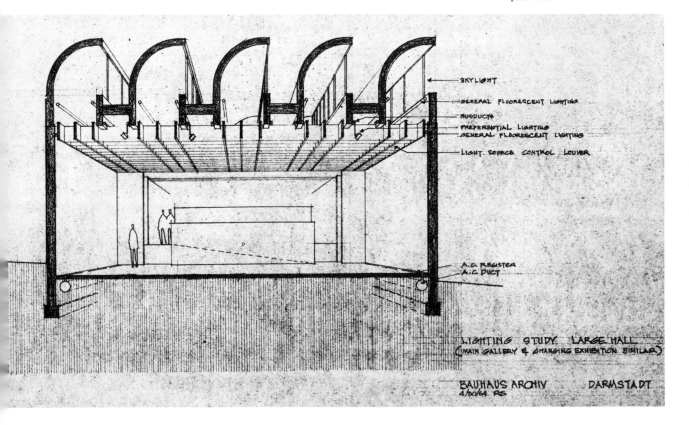

SKYLIGHT
GENERAL FLUORESCENT LIGHTING
BUSDUCTS
PREFERENTIAL LIGHTING
GENERAL FLUORESCENT LIGHTING
LIGHT SOURCE CONTROL LOUVER

A.C. REGISTER
A.C. DUCT

LIGHTING STUDY LARGE HALL
(MAIN GALLERY & CHANGING EXHIBITION SIMILAR)

BAUHAUS ARCHIV   DARMSTADT
4/30/64 RS

building parts, shell constructions, stilts under buildings, and ribbon windows are some of the very elements of contemporary building technique. They influence, of course, the form of buildings today as much as the structural inventions of vaults, domes, and arches influenced the periods of their first appearance. Structural systems are the means of realizing architectural visions. Their very medium is space itself. But as the science of building has its language of materials and construction, the science of space has a grammar all its own. For instance, compare the physical qualities of an actually built room, that is to say, the work of the engineer and the builder, with the appearance of the room as it is intended by its designer. Whereas the technician has to follow the law of gravity, the designer works, in addition, with a totally different set of laws and rules which condition the surface appearance. In fact, in his desire to create psychological effects, he can produce illusions which seem to belie the facts of measurement and construction. Color and texture of surfaces have an effective existence of their own, sending out physical and psychological energies which can be measured as such. The effect can be either warm or cold, advancing or receding, bright or dark, tension or suspension, and even attractive or repulsive.

Ignorance or disregard of the "science of space," as I would like to call it, keeps many designers from reaching the threshold of true architecture. The well-known process of pseudodesign, namely, piecing together rooms according to their use value and having them dressed up stylistically, misses the essence of a space creation which would deserve the name architecture. *True architecture is the creation of new living space for man; its aim is to offer a "life in space" in full relationship with it, rather than a retreat from space in a fixed enclosure.* When the functions of all parts of a building have been put into well-selected relationships by its designer, a spacial equilibrium of taut forces, held well in balance, will result. If, going into and around such an edifice, we find a consistent composition of spatial surprises, then we experience the marvel of pure, equipoised architecture.

The study of objectively valid optical facts will guide the designer from observation to knowledge, from experience to intuition. In music, a composer is bound to use counterpoint as a key common to all;

its mastery is required lest the musical idea remain lost in chaos. Bach's *Well-Tempered Clavichord* is still the prevailing common denominator for our Western music. Of course, mastery of counterpoint does not make a composer a genius. However, it is an indispensable auxiliary for his creative work and helps the listener to understand it.

In the optical arts, there existed formerly an elaborate counterpoint of space as, for instance, in the Greek, Indian, and Gothic architecture. There was, for instance, the Gothic system of triangulation and the module system of the Greeks; but those design keys have been lost. The Academy, whose task should have been from the Middle Ages, when it was still a vital force, to tend and develop this counterpoint or space system of the optical arts, failed because it lost touch with reality and with the people. It was left to our period to rediscover the grammar of design and to redevelop it. At least we are able today to underpin the designer's creative talent with the knowledge of physical facts, such as the phenomena of optical illusions, of space and volume, of light and shade, of color and scale—objective facts instead of arbitrary subjective whims and fancies or of formulas long-since stale. Many of these facts are of psychological origin, but they must be considered as real as physical facts. Striking evidence to support such a statement comes with the following test.

Standing high up on a balcony with an open railing, many of us experience a sensation of dizziness. Such dizziness stops immediately, however, when cardboard or paper is hung on that open railing which, giving the eye support, reestablishes our equilibrium through the *illusion* of safety, though of course nothing has been added for greater physical safety.

This example shows the power of space illusions and the part they may play in architecture.

Science defines space as "the relation between the position of bodies." The effect of an architectural or sculptural work of art results from the juxtaposition of bodies and of the empty spaces in and around them. We can observe that the contemporary architect is in search of a new space–time relation—judging from his attempts to create kinetic illusions, that is, the illusion of motion in static space as a stimulant. We experience today a preference for transparency in buildings, for using large areas of glass, for undercutting and opening up parts of the buildings to achieve a floating continuity of space. Space seems to move in and out of the building, and sections of the infinite outdoor space become a definite part of the architect's space composition, which does not stop at the enclosing exterior walls, but is carried beyond them into the open.

A solid wall prevents the eye from looking into the neighboring space. An open frame, however, with stretched wire mesh, a piece of trellis, a glass pane, or only the edge of a terrace will suffice just to outline wall-less space volumes which may interpenetrate each other as well as the solid parts of the building. The building has tentacles, so to speak, with which to embrace part of the outer space; indoor and outdoor space together become one indivisible entity, both as an artistic composition and as a diversified receptacle of life. By such means, systems of coordinates in space are established which help the eye to grasp the delineation of the space units and their mutual relationships as they have been intended by the designer. The creation of such a masterly framework of coordinates in space depends on the designer's artistic sensibility, and on his capacity to think three-dimensionally.

A good contemporary museum building should show a balanced combination of the best available at present in the social, psychological, technical, and economic fields. As modern science is always replacing earlier human discoveries which, in their time, stirred the imagination of their contemporaries, but have now lost their relative truthfulness, so does the human mind go on changing its *Weltanschauung,* and this process is mirrored in the image of its representative buildings.

Theater Design

Address given at "Volta Congress,"
Reale Accademia d'Italia,
Rome, 1934

63. "Total Theater," Walter Gropius. 1927.
Model. View into the auditorium. The "Total
Theater" was designed for Erwin Piscator,
theater director in Berlin. The auditorium was
planned for 2,000 seats amphitheatrically
arranged. The project provided a stage in arena
form, a proscenium stage and a backstage, the
latter divisible into three parts. If desirable,
the transformation could take place even during
a performance. Film projections on screens,
hung between the twelve columns surrounding
the auditorium, were to provide the scenery for
the arena stage. As a result of this arrangement,
the spectator would sit amidst the dramatic
happening and its imaginary world.

Theater Design

A theater building and its architecture form the spatial vessel for the whole scope of dramatic action; the multiple requirements of theatrical performances determine its type of construction.

I believe that a purge and renewal of the theater—a theater that has lost its intimate emotional relationship to man, when compared to the great cultures of the past—are possible only by a fundamental clarification of all the problems of stagecraft in their theoretical and practical aspects as they relate to the slowly emerging image of our new society. For theater is a mirror of life. It can be the voice of all, transcending the confines of any one class, only by discovering the magic formula that will touch the heart of all levels of society.

Basically, the stage arose from a metaphysical longing and serves to give form to transcendental ideas. Its impact upon the heart of the spectator depends upon the success of translating an idea into palpable

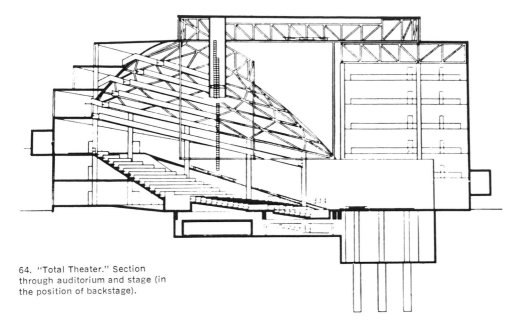

64. "Total Theater." Section through auditorium and stage (in the position of backstage).

form—speech, sound, and space. Of course, the literary work of the poet and the musical work of the composer lie beyond the scope of this report, which will deal only with clarifying the architectural requirements as they arise from the spatial demands of the stage production.

The phenomenon of spatial experience evolves from the creation of finite limits within infinite space, the motion of mechanical and organic bodies, and the play of light and sound within these confines. The creation of dramatic, animated (that is, artistic) space presupposes a mastery of statics, mechanics, optics, and acoustics.

Thus formulated, the path toward a rebirth of the theater is clear. We must investigate the various problems of space, matter, form, color, light, movement, and sound; develop the movements of organic and mechanical bodies; develop speech, musical and mechanical sounds; study the development of stage design, figures, and lighting. The same optical, acoustical, and mechanical laws will hold for all types of the performing arts and their relative scale, be they philosophical or entertaining in nature, drama or *variété*.

The stage play is essentially a collective undertaking. Out of its complex nature arise its many individual problems, each one representing its own realm of artistic relevance. The impact of a play depends, therefore, upon a director's coordinating the individual performances of actors, musicians, dancers, stage designers, and technicians. For all of them a literary or a musical play is, so to speak, but a means for demonstrating their own intuitive skills; their individual performances do not exist per se, but assume meaning only as a common enterprise.

The multiplicity of problems in any stage production explains the rarity of a superb director, a director whose talents must encompass all artistic areas. He must be a universal man. The decisive factor in any great performance is his ability and talent, even if he can count on the best actors and specialists. His imagination alone can unify a production.

I view the task of the contemporary theater architect as that of creating a great keyboard for light and space for such a universal director. This should be so impersonal and variable that it will not restrict him in the least, but will respond to any vision of his imagination—a flexible building, capable of transforming and refreshing the mind by its spatial impact alone.

How can the architect aid in ending the stagnation that has overtaken the theater and in giving new impulses to the producer who suffers from a lack of new ideas in theater construction? The stage is the heart of a theater building. Its type and location in relation to the spectator are decisive for the way the unfolding action affects the audience by pictorial intensity and spatial revelations. It is from here that the search for a new form of playhouse must start.

History knows only three basic kinds of stage. The first one and most elemental was the central circular stage, the arena of antiquity. Here the stage unfolded three dimensionally and was seen from all sides by an audience sitting concentrically around this arena. The actor here was the exponent of the masses; he was its captive united with it as gladiator, priest, orator, or artist. Today we know this three-dimensional theater only in the form of sports, bullfighting, and circus arenas. Whereas some Asians have retained its form as a dance and play podium in the midst of surrounding throngs, Europe has cultivated almost exclusively the stage behind apron and curtain.

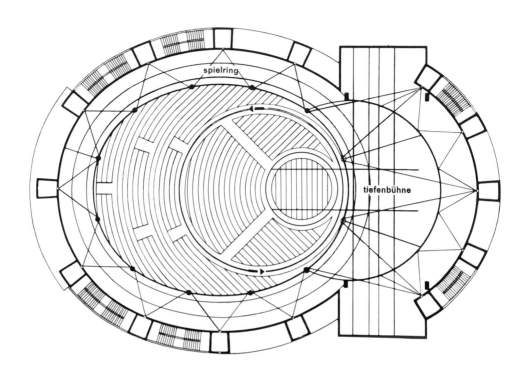

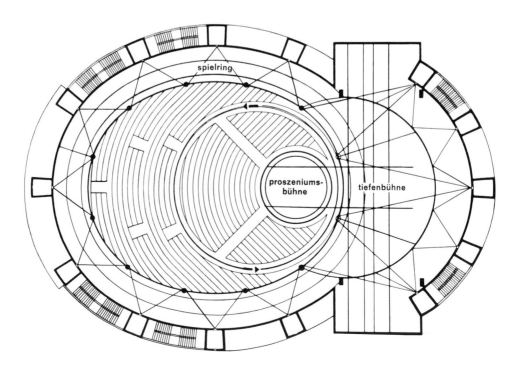

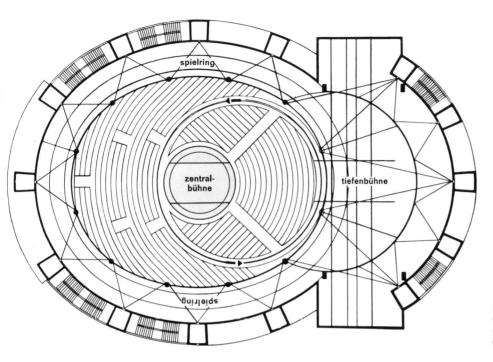

The labels within the image read:
spielring, zentral-bühne, tiefenbühne, spielring

65. "Total Theater." Plans of the three stage variations: backstage (top left), proscenium stage (bottom left), arena stage (above).

The second classical stage of antiquity was the Greek proscenium theater with semicircularly arranged spectator seats embracing a projecting forestage or proscenium. A play was not seen from all around as it was on the arena stage, but rather in relief form, beyond a semicircular stage facing front, right, and left, but against a solid background for actors' entrances and exits. This background—also the place of emergence of a *deus ex machina*—marks the end of the stage in free space, since now every spatial movement of the drama, every step and gesture of the actor was related to this fixed wall, to the background surface of the relief-like moving scene, the plane from which backdrops, wings, and curtains have later developed.

This back wall of the open relief-type proscenium stage eventually receded more and more from the spectator, being sucked in to form the deep stage, the "peep show" that dominates contemporary theater. A basically new space creation—the third and last stage form—thus arose. The locale of reality, the world of the spectator, was separated from the locale of illusion, i.e., the world of the actor. The spectator now gazes from his own profane setting on one side of the curtain through a framed window-like opening beyond, to the shifting scenes of a world of make-believe which the curtain unveils. The plasticity of the third dimension is now reduced to the flatness of a picture on a photographic focusing screen, and the spectator is no longer physically involved in the vibrations and gyrations of the play. Banned beyond the footlights, his active participation shrinks with the loss of being spatially included in the play; he stands now beside the drama, not within it. This spatial separation of the world of the viewer from that of the actor—no matter how much technical perfection it may have brought—has unfortunately limited the spectator to experiencing the play on an intellectual level only.

Thus did the "court theater" that dominates unchallenged today gradually replace the early theater of the participating audience. With the former's boxes, upholstered stalls, and galleries, the idea of spatial differentiation between stage and auditorium was carried over into the seating arrangement. Society itself became a sideshow and degraded the stage play to mere aesthetic entertainment. The conventional theater that followed that of the court altered the process only by ranking wealth above class, and the commercial theater, which maintained the conventional deep stage and seating arrangement, gradually lost whatever attachment the people still had for it in spite of its lavish displays. Indeed, modern man came to believe that he didn't even need the theater any more, that it could be replaced by films which were closer to world events. The stage *form* had become obsolete, and it was believed that the stage itself had become so. The baby was thrown out with the wash. The theater lost its impact as soon as it lost sight of its original capacity to enthrall and activate an audience by spatial means; unless it can recapture this magic, it will continue to lose ground to movies.

But what kind of stage should a modern director seek? Every type is historically valid; every age created the dramatic forum it needed. We must simply recognize that the amphitheater of antiquity as well as the late classical stage of Terence, the two-level stage of the Middle Ages as well as that of Elizabethan England and the typical court stage; all have timeless values that can be combined into a new space form for the theater of the future. None of the three classic types (round, relief, or deep stage) can suffice alone; only their sum can meet the spatial requirements of a future stage production that again will engage and rouse the masses by using all realistic and transcendental theatrical possibilities inherent in speech, music, dance, sport, and film, that will be sustained again by its direct relevance to the motivating forces of our time.

The theater of the future must become a spiritual center for the masses, fulfilling its social and dramatic role. To this end it must be an architectural totality. Stage and auditorium will be one, each part accentuated, but not separated from the other.

The public must be rooted from its intellectual apathy, assaulted, and forced to participate in the play

By employing all spatial techniques

By linking stage and auditorium

By carrying action into the auditorium, surrounding and penetrating the audience until it becomes part of it and cannot escape behind the curtain

By making the spectator take part in processions and parades

By inventing space illusions

By animating the entire theater three dimensionally, replacing the flat pictorial aspect of the conventional deep stage

By incorporating mechanical lighting devices that can sweep the darkened theater in all directions and transform it to suit the visions of the director

By utilizing projection equipment that will enable the director to turn walls and ceiling into movie screens, i.e., to build his scene with light and thereby reduce also painted scenery and massive props. The sum total of all these projection *planes* will produce a three-dimensional *space* composition. The auditorium itself—dissolved into a transmutable illusionary space—becomes the place of action

By making the technical stage into a precision instrument of mechanical functions not unlike an industrial assembly line, or a railroad yard, a central command post from which to control all motions and lighting functions as simply and flexibly as possible

By making any scenery that might still be required readily portable without need of a cumbersome system of tracks

A network of aisles should make it possible for actors to cross the playhouse to and from the stage, either individually or in groups, as in processions. These latter can be facilitated by openings at both sides of the stage.

Vision and acoustics must be excellent in all parts of the theater. This will necessitate shortening the length of the auditorium so that it is at most as large as the large European opera houses without at the same time narrowing the width of the auditorium. This will tend to make the theater circular or oval.

To avoid steep angles of vision, there should be no more than one balcony, nor should parts of the audience be isolated in unconnected areas.

The playhouse must permit quick entry and exit via short connecting aisles leading to the exits at the periphery. Escalators and ramps should take the place of stairways to the balcony; the checkroom should have a broad and open face. The vestibule and foyer should be combined as one large room for the intermissions.

And the architecture of the new theater? It will be a tremendous demonstration of everything that our age has created in new construction techniques and new materials. Glass, concrete, steel, and other metals will be used, harmonized by the laws of proportion, rhythm, and the color and structure of the materials. Instead of facades in borrowed styles and overelaborate interior decoration, we should concentrate on pure relation between material and abstract space, on creating a noble edifice for the inherent power of drama. In this sense, the architect actually becomes the very creator of the theater, just as the stage form itself will call forth new types of plays from the playwright. For even as spirit shapes matter, so can a building transform the spirit and stimulate the spatial imagination of the author.

Our time is very poor in examples of determined advances in the realm of theatrical production. The sole attempts at revitalizing the stagnating conventional deep stage, breaking up the flatness of it by beginning to reconquer a third dimension, were made by Van de Velde with his tripartite stage in Cologne in 1914 (subsequently further developed by Perret in 1925 for the Theater of the Arts and Crafts Exhibition in Paris), and by Poelzig with his remodeling of Reinhardt's Grosses Schauspielhaus, which includes a proscenium projecting far beyond the current line. The time is yet to come for the still bolder stage designs of Strnad in Vienna, the brothers Wessnin, and Golosow in Russia, Kiessler and Kastner in the United States, Zdenko von Strizic and Traugott Müller in Berlin, and myself.

As an example, I will describe more fully a theater I designed which comes closest to the basic demands of the future stage, as I have outlined them.

In my "Total Theater"—originally conceived for Erwin Piscator—I attempted to create a theatrical instrument so flexible that a director could apply all three classical stage types—circular, proscenium, and deep-stage—under one roof with the aid of some simple, ingenious mechanisms.

The ground plan of the theater is elliptical and its section a parabolic curve in keeping with the demands for good acoustics. The plan of the theater resembles an egg, cut in half lengthwise, with a tripartite deep stage at one end. The combination of a revolving stage with two staggered stage carts, corresponding to the width of the center opening and to be entered from the sides, permits an exceptional number of combinations. These flat stage carts can be used for choral purposes and may be driven around the circumferential concourse. The stalls, arranged amphitheatrically, are not bordered by boxes and encircle, pincer-like, the circular proscenium which can be, in itself, raised or lowered. This raisable stage is, at the same time, built off-center into a larger turntable that holds the first rows of spectators. An actor can thereby descend into the audience or mount the stage in any number of ways. There are three circular aisles through and around the theater, which can be used for theatrical demonstrations and processions. The first ring surrounds the proscenium stage, the second the large turntable, and the third one runs around the whole auditorium behind the interior columns supporting the building.

A complete transformation of the theater takes place, though, when the large turntable stage is turned 180° around its center point. The built-in proscenium stage then becomes an arena in the center of the auditorium, surrounded by spectators on all sides. This movement can even be accomplished during a performance. Actors can enter this arena either from below by stairs or by the aisle leading back to the deepstage (when the proscenium disc is in this position) or even from above by ladders or similar apparatus to be lowered from the ceiling. This will then also permit vertical action above the arena.

This assault on the spectator, dislodging him and unexpectedly shifting the center of action to another location, suspends conventional expectations and makes him an active participant in the drama by thrusting him physically into another spatial context.

At the same time, the darkened theater is being transformed into the scenic background of the play. Its dome and walls are bathed in light by films projected from cameras placed at the center and on the periphery of the house. The spectator sits under clouds or stars, surrounded by waves of the sea or by masses of people charging at him from all sides, while the dramatic action in the arena holds him captive. The separation of spectacle and spectator has been overcome! Speech, light, and music are no longer fixed in their position. The director reigns supreme and dictates the foci of interest as the play demands. He can shift the place of action and its spatial context and has the audience at the mercy of his dynamic imagery.

The goal of this Total Theater is to overwhelm the spectator. All technical devices serve this goal; but they must never become an end in themselves. The simpler and more efficient, the less chance is there for them to get out of the hand of the creative director. It makes as little sense to fight against stage mechanics as to overdo them. The expenditure for such a flexible stage mechanism would be fully compensated for by the diversity of purposes to which such a transformable building would lend itself: the presentation of drama, opera, film, and dance; choral or instrumental music; sports events or conventions.

The Total Theater is a new type of a theater for large audiences. Smaller theaters do not have to differ from it basically—only in degree. The same laws, experiences, and spatial conceptions apply there as well.

But how can we make progress without constructing new theaters? Where are our clients? I believe that, first of all, the government should take the initiative as patron of a people's cultural life in giving new impetus to a now stagnant theater through promoting a fresh approach to theater building. Just think of the gap that exists between the contemporary commercial theater and the state-supported classical theater of Greece! No new life can come from the conventionally organized playhouse. I propose the state-supported experimental theater. Can we not find the initiators who will forward the cause of the theater in our changing society?

66. Le Corbusier (right) talking with Walter and Ise Gropius, Paris, 1930. The meeting took place during the Werkbund Exhibition in the "Salon des Artistes Decorateurs," arranged by Gropius.

67. Peter Behrens

Encounters

Peter Behrens

From 1907 to 1910, Peter Behrens was my master who introduced me to the problems of design and architecture. He gave me the first foundation on which later on I could build up my own development as an architect. His comprehensive and penetrating interest in the total environment, in many-sided fields of design—building, stagework, industrial products, printing, and layout work—greatly attracted me. For three years I worked closely with him on many of his projects, learning from his systematic approach to design and from his mastery of the tectonic, of architectural space, and of proportion. He drew my attention to the stereometric secrets of the medieval mason guilds and to the geometric system of Greek architecture. We often went together to see the buildings of Friedrich Schinkel in and around Potsdam, in whom he saw his artistic ancestor.

He was an imposing personality, well dressed and having the cool deportment of a conservative Hamburg patrician. Endowed with will power and a penetrating intellect, he was moved more by reason than by emotion, but he took a fresh, unprejudiced start for any problem of design.

I owe him much, particularly the habit of thinking in principles.

On Frank Lloyd Wright

Frank Lloyd Wright was very well known and respected in Europe long before he gained a reputation in the United States. When the Academy of Arts in Berlin arranged an exhibition of Frank Lloyd Wright's work in 1911, and the publishing house of Wasmuth, Berlin subsequently published a portfolio of it, I first became attracted to his strong, imaginative approach. I still remember that I was impressed by the Larkin Building in Buffalo and by the Robie House in Chicago, both of which were close to my own thinking and feeling. Their straight-forwardness of unconventional design fascinated me, while I was less attracted by the romanticism of many of his residential buildings.

At this time I had just designed the Fagus Factory in Alfeld a. d. Leine. My acquaintance with Wright's work clarified my own approach and helped me to become more articulate in defining my own design philosophy.

When I came to the United States for the first time on a visit in 1928, almost nobody appreciated Wright's work except a few personal admirers. It was almost impossible even to start a conversation about him, because his architectural deeds were at that time completely overshadowed by scandalous newspaper gossip about his private life. In the AIA he was considered to be an "immoral crank." However, I managed to see and photograph quite a few of his buildings in Chicago and Los Angeles, which I then used frequently for my lectures on architecture in Germany.

When I returned to the United States in 1937 to become Chairman of the Department of Architecture of the Harvard Graduate School of Design, I still found such a vast ignorance about Wright's work among my students and the public that I undertook to open their eyes to his brilliant work and to his historic importance, in public lectures and in discussions in the School.

In 1940, Wright came to Boston to deliver a lecture. He accepted an invitation to my house in Lincoln, Massachusetts, and we had a few undisturbed hours of free conversation, during which he complained bitterly about the treatment he had received in his own country. He referred particularly to the fact that I had been made Chairman of the Department of Architecture at Harvard, whereas he himself had never been offered such a position of influence when he was younger. He believed seriously that I had been given every advantage and every opportunity in my life and my career that anybody could wish for. He seemed quite baffled when I told him that the modern European architects, including myself, had run into much greater obstacles in obtaining any commissions at all than he had ever had to contend with.

His self-centeredness was irritating and at the same time disarming, for he was hiding his hurt feelings behind a mask of haughty arrogance which gradually became his second nature. The students at Harvard who had hoped to have a question and answer period with him soon found that they were only at the receiving end.

In subsequent years, Wright conducted an aggressive campaign against the so-called "international style" which he sensed to become a challenge to his own.

In 1947, I met Wright again at Princeton University at the "Bicentennial Conference on Planning Man's Physical Surroundings" and again in 1955 in Mexico City. The Mexican government had invited both of us to be present at the opening of their new University. The Mexican–German architect, Max Cetto, with whom I was staying, gave an evening to which he invited leading Mexican architects and also Frank Lloyd Wright. Just before Wright arrived, I talked to my colleagues about collaborative teams in our profession. When Wright entered, he sat at my side and smilingly encouraged me to go ahead. When I had finished, he said: "But, Walter, when you want to make a child you don't ask for the help of your neighbor." Thinking fast I countered: "If the neighbor happens to be a woman, I might." Frank laughed, and this was the only time I managed to have the last word in skirmishes with the quick-witted master. This was also my last personal meeting with him.

Wright's notorious opposition to the Bauhaus had, I believe, its origin in their widely differing conception of the educational process. This may become evident when I compare our methods of approach in educating students. Wright, ingenious, inventive artist and full of stimulating ideas, followed his conception that a style of the century could be achieved by disseminating his own personal vocabulary of

68. Frank Lloyd Wright (left) talking with Walter and Ise Gropius at the opening of the Bauhaus Exhibition in the Museum of Modern Art, New York, 1938.

form. His school in Taliesin, Wisconsin was meant to consolidate his own form pattern into a universal style. In 1961, I visited his school, which his widow valiantly carried on after his death. There I saw the work of several scores of students turning out, without exception, designs in the vocabulary of their great master. I did not see any independent design. This autocratic method of approach cannot be called creative, for it invites imitation; it results in training assistants, not independent artists. Surely the contact of the student with a radiating personality like Frank Lloyd Wright must have been an invaluable and unforgettable experience, but here I try to compare educational methods and goals which must not be confounded with the artistic potency of the teacher. A great architect does not necessarily develop an effective educational method.

Already in the Bauhaus, I had come to the conclusion that an autocratic, subjective approach must block the innate budding expression of differently gifted students, if the teacher, even with the best intentions, imposes the results of his own thought and work on them. We tried, therefore, on the contrary, to discourage imitation of the teacher, and help the student to observe and understand physical and psychological facts and from there let him find his own way. Here, then, I differ in principle from Wright's approach to education which strikes me as being wholly egocentric. But from this strong emphasis on his ego originated also his superb if somewhat upsetting showmanship which, there can be no doubt, has helped to bring the course of architecture into the public's consciousness.

69. Ludwig Mies van der Rohe, 1931.

Laudatio for Ludwig Mies van der Rohe

Ludwig Mies van der Rohe grew up in Aachen, early capital of the Franco–German empire, amidst beautiful medieval architecture. A son of a stonemason, he learned his father's craft and simultaneously became influenced by the profound spirit of the great medieval thinkers and writers Thomas Aquinas and St. Augustine, whose words "Beauty is the splendor of truth" struck roots in him. On the lonely and thorny way to world fame as a great creative architect, Mies' strength of character has contributed as much to his success as his innate artistic talents. His famous slogan "Less is more," coined when he had already become a mature master in this country, expresses in three syllables the long, exhausting effort it must have taken him to penetrate to the essentials of design by resolutely discarding, discarding—everything superfluous. As a lonely seeker of truth, engaging all his spiritual and intellectual qualities with utter disregard for success or failure, he very slowly has acquired authority, but only after what had become a long struggle.

Address given on the occasion of the presentation of the Gold Medal of the National Institute of Arts and Letters and the American Academy of Arts and Letters, New York, May, 1963

Half a century ahead of his time, almost unnoticed, Mies created right after World War I, with unequaled consistency and daring, a sequence of bold designs of uncompromising directness. His innovations contributed to the new set of values for architectural design which have become characteristic of today's architecture.

Capable of thinking in principles, Mies steadily pursued his aim to reach ever-greater simplicity and purity of design, reduced to the essentials of structure and envelopment, of "skin and bones" as he calls it. His new conception of the function of the wall reveals how his imagination works: by juxtaposition of wall slabs and large glassed apertures he tends to let indoors and outdoors float into each other. His additional notion of "universal space" creates new horizons for flexibility.

This disciplined process of Mies, the artist, relentlessly distilling the permanent from the transitory and fashionable and "giving the spirit opportunity of existence" attaches an appeal of poetry to his creations. He seeks God in the excellence of proportion, detail, and craftsmanship, but he denies a preconception of form.

The artistic integrity of Mies van der Rohe's architectural work reveals its truth in shiny buildings which have become beautiful landmarks of our time. They give a silent lesson of how human discipline and equipoise may overcome the ugliness and disorder of our amorphous urban scene. A rare and happy combination of the most prominent gifts of heart and mind puts Mies van der Rohe in the front line of the great masters· of the past. Through his fundamental achievements, he belongs to the world and will belong to history.

Igor Stravinsky

I met Stravinsky for the first time when the Bauhaus in Weimar invited him to be present during its festival in 1923, at a performance of his "Histoire d'un Soldat." The first performance had just taken place in Frankfurt am Main with Hermann Scherchen as conductor, who brought the whole cast with Karl Ebert as "narrator" to the theater in Jena, which I had just rebuilt. This first meeting established my admiration for his art and his personality.

Again I saw him in Frankfurt during a rehearsal of his "Persephone," under Klemperer. I still remember Stravinsky exhorting the orchestra members: "Don't offer the audience *your* emotions on a platter! You should call forth *their* emotions!"

Later, as a member of the architectural faculty of Harvard University I succeeded in persuading my dean to propose Stravinsky for the Charles Eliot Norton Professorship, endowed with $12,000 at that time. The proposal was accepted, and Stravinsky came for several months to Harvard, lecturing and conducting his works. He stayed on in the United States after that and became the brilliant center of a creative music circle in California.

We both owe a debt to our adopted country for a new chance at life at a time when the European continent was darkened, and its cultural life was running in ever narrower channels.

70. Igor Stravinsky. From a visit by Stravinsky in Lincoln, Mass.
Photo: Walter Gropius.

Memories of Le Corbusier

In 1923, when I prepared the Bauhaus Exhibition in Weimar, Germany, my friendship with Le Corbusier began. From his *Esprit Nouveau,* I was familiar with his philosophy. Attracted by it, I asked him to send me samples of his work to be shown in the Exhibition and later in the first volume of the Bauhaus Books, which I published under the title *Internationale Architektur.* He responded enthusiastically and sent me handwritten summaries and sketches of his studies for city planning and for prefabrication, as well as photos of the very few houses he had built as yet.

After the Bauhaus Exhibition, we met for the first time in Paris in the Café des Deux Magots and discussed his plans for a *ville contemporaine de 3,000,000* (*Esprit Nouveau,* 1922) and the idea of standardization and prefabrication of houses which we both were highly interested in at that time. I also gave him photos of American silos which I had collected and published in the *Werkbund Yearbook,* 1913, and which he republished in his *Vers une Architecture.* He took me to see two houses he had built for Ozenfant, the painter, and Maison la Roche; the fresh design approach for both greatly excited me.

After his housing colony in Pessac near Bordeaux was built in 1925, I went down there to see it. Enthusiastic about the abundance of ideas and the poetic beauty of their embodiment with simple means, I told Corbu about my reactions. It was then that our friendship became solid, for he had found only very little popular response and felt bitter about it. Such bitterness persecuted him to the very end. He was too passionate, too convinced of his mission to content himself with the all-too-few opportunities given to him to show his architectural genius. Whenever I saw him in later years, he complained to me about the absence of due recognition, charging it to the fact that he was too much ahead of his time.

From 1929 to 1934, we met regularly in the Congrès Internationaux d'Architecture Moderne, CIAM, in Frankfurt, Brussels, Berlin, Barcelona, Aix-en-Provence, and London. Corbu exercised the greatest influence at these meetings. The final result of CIAM *La Charte d'Athenes* greatly followed his own formulations.

When I assembled the Werkbund Exhibition in Paris, 1930, in Le Salon des Artistes Decorateurs, I persuaded the German Ambassador to give a large reception in his Embassy, the beautiful Palais Beauharnais. This turned into a very gay evening, attended by the French *avant garde,* among them Corbu, Perret, Léger, and, of course, the exhibiting Bauhaus artists, Moholy-Nagy, Marcel Breuer, Herbert Bayer, and myself. I never saw Corbu in higher spirits, laughing and joking in a, for him, so rare carefree mood.

During the war, I lost sight of him, but, when the UNESCO nominated an international Committee of five to advise them on their headquarters building in Paris, I was again to come close to Corbu and to get firsthand, intimate knowledge of his personality. This Committee of five consisted of Corbu (France), Sven Markelius (Sweden), Lucio Costa (Brazil), Ernesto Rogers (Italy), and myself (United States). I took over the Chairmanship.

The veto of the United States delegation had wrecked Corbu's legitimate chances to become the architect for the UNESCO Building even before our Committee of five was installed. But since the Committee members were unanimous in the approach to their advisory task, I saw the possibility of using our influence at the Quai d'Orsay and at the Board of UNESCO. However, our vigorous attempt to intercede in favor of Corbu bogged down, for we were instructed that international custom did not permit reconsideration of his candidacy after he had already accepted membership in our Committee, unaware of the consequences this would imply. He felt deeply offended to have been passed over again, as had happened before for reasons of ignorance and intrigue after he had won the First Prize in the competition for the Palais des Nations in Geneva but was not commissioned with the execution, and again when, under pressure of an unsympathetic setup, he lost the leadership for the design of the United Nations Building in New York. Naturally his depression about this new loss of the UNESCO Building was abysmal. Slowly and carefully I tried, together with Rogers, to eliminate his negative attitude and to keep him active in the work of our Committee. During a long evening with him and his wife, Yvonne, in his Paris flat, I finally succeeded in winning him over to cooperate again with our Committee, which he did loyally from then on. The next day he sent me a painting of his, which I had admired, with a warm and touching letter, my proud possession, which reads:

Dear Gropius,

I think I noticed that you like this little painting. Let me offer it to you. I love it much myself; it is one of my best; it was painted during the Occupation's grievous days.

I have passed two happy weeks at your side. I have appreciated and admired you, feeling true and respectful for you. I say *"respectful."* This is to signify that the reasons for my appreciation are profound.

The fruit of our work, the CIAM, seems to be ripening. That's why the fruits fall. The mature fruits, that's us! Happy maturity! It is the rule that fruits are consumed, particularly if they are good! You have had an exemplary and fruitful career; around you art and spirit flourish among the youth; you are loved by all.

By me too.

Yours Corbu

Here speaks Baudelaire: "Be wise my grief,
contain yourself. . . ."
Let's date this line
UNESCO, Paris, May 13, 1952
Since I am at poetry I enclose one line of my Poem "The Right Angle," edited in 1950–52

The words of Baudelaire which Corbu quotes at the end of this letter characterize his state of mind then and thereafter. His wife died in 1957, and I saw Corbu shortly after in Bagdad where we both had negotiations about building projects with the Iraqi Government. When I entered his hotel room, he burst into tears and threw his arms around me. I found him then to be the loneliest man, desolate about the loss of his companion who was a down-to-earth woman he had greatly respected.

In all his actions he was most genuinely direct, but this often looked like an offense to others even when it was not meant that way. I see no point in counting the difficulties one encountered in dealing with him personally, as, for example, his errors in judgment of people and circumstances brought about by his autarchic self-absorption. The important thing is that he did not err before history. His shortcomings were only inevitable counterpoints to his enormous gifts, and one could only accept—or reject—his total personality.

As surprising and spectacular as his ideas have been, his physical

71. Le Corbusier (center), Walter Gropius, Marcel Breuer (standing), and Sven Markelius at a session during the construction of the UNESCO Building, Paris, 1952. Le Corbusier, Gropius, and Markelius were members of the international advisory "Committee of Five," together with Lucio Costa and Ernesto Rogers. The UNESCO Building was executed according to the plans by Marcel Breuer, Pier Luigi Nervi, and Bernard Zehrfuss after they had been approved by the "Committee of Five."

requirements for living were plain and unpretentious. For many years he dined in Paris in a tiny, primitive restaurant in St.-Germain-des-Prés. For years he drove around in a ramshackle little green car—his "frog." His private room in his studio in Rue de Sèvres was a small cubbyhole where he could reach each wall by hand from his seat. His two-room bachelor house in Cap Martin where he died was similarly a minimum abode, all the details of which he once explained to me with true excitement, for his mind was always occupied with the idea of achieving simple efficiency, poetically expressed. He was seeking the paradox which speaks to the imagination.

It is difficult to fathom the implications of his lifework. The moment he disappeared beyond recall from our limited field of vision, the full impact and weight of his great and noble personality came to my mind with a flash. How tragic that he could not live out his immeasurable potentialities, that he had to break off before the reasons for his state of bitterness about the true and imagined slighting of his person could have been removed. France remains in debt. Still, Claudius Petit saw early the greatness of Le Corbusier and exposed himself by publicly supporting him when he was Minister of Reconstruction.

The balance of his life—a prolific abundance of architecture, of poetry, of inventiveness—characterizes the work and life of this universal man. He gave the world a new visual vocabulary, profound enough to enrich generations to come. In every field of urban planning and architecture, he offered basic answers and renewed his messages by ever-fresh, surprising creations. The new images he blessed us with will endure.

Index